Truman's Birthplace
Lamar, Missouri

By Reba Young

Pelican Publishing Company
Gretna 2004

Copyright © 1992
By The Lamar Democrat

Copyright © 2004
By Mike and Teresa Young
All rights reserved

First edition, 1992
First Pelican edition, 2004

Printed in the United States of America

Published by Pelican Publishing Company, Inc.
1000 Burmaster Street, Gretna, Louisiana 70053

Index

Dedication

With love to my two children, Robert K. Young and Marian Young Davies and to my good friend, Doug Davis.

My Thanks

My sincere thanks to the entire staff of The Lamar Democrat for printing my articles on Barton County History.

I appreciate the searching of records that J. D. Phalow did for me. My friend, Edith Klein, was a big help in recalling earlier day facts. The assistance Helen Satterlee gave in preparing the articles for the printer was valuable and most appreciated. Without the encouragement and help of these folks and many others (including Elaine Brannon) this book might never have been printed.

Introduction

I was born in very early 1901 and have seen practically a century of change in my lifetime. There were no radios or television; no cars and certainly no airplanes. When I was small our traveling was by horse and buggy. This era has seen more changes than any previous century. It has been a privilege to live and experience this time on God's earth.

The Author

Reba and husband, Charles.

Our Civil War Cannon

March 24, 1980

How many of you living here today know the story about the old cannon in the northeast part of our courtyard?

Just recently when I was preparing a program on "Barton County and Lamar of Yore" I ran across the complete account in a small booklet published in 1915 by Dr. W.L. Griffin exactly 50 years after the close of the Civil War. It is titled "All Soldiers and Soldier's Widows in Barton County." Since Missouri was a divided state, we here in Barton County ran true to form and also had veterans on both sides in the war. In this booklet each veteran and all veteran's widows who were living here in 1915 wrote of their service experiences and a bit of what had happened to them since the war.

One of the Union Veterans was a Mr. Allen Cockrell who, when I was a little girl, lived in the two story house on the southeast corner of 13th and Mill Street. After the war was over, he purchased the old cannon from a junk pile in St. Louis and had it brought to Lamar.

For many years, it stood either at the old Fair grounds near where the Vo-Tech School now is, or somewhere adjacent to the public square. It had been used to fire salutes on their reunion and rally days, on the Fourth of July and on what was then called Decoration Day. The purpose was to keep green the memories of the days when it did its deadly work as a war weapon.

In the summer of 1910 it was decided to spike its tube, seal its mouth and mount it in the Courthouse park where it still stands today, a silent reminder of those tragic days. A dedication service was planned with an appropriate ceremony.

Mr. Willard O. Walters, grandfather of Allen Walters, our local photographer, suggested that a picture be taken during the dedication with the "Old Boys" in blue standing on one side of the cannon and the "Old Boys" in Gray on the other. Each reached across to grasp the hand of the former enemy while the picture was taken by C. R. Taylor.

My mother had sent me to town that day to buy some meat at the butcher shop on the north side of the square. I saw this picture taken and even though I was only nine years old, I remember the event vividly. I can't help wondering if I am now the only living person who witnessed this historic event. As I look at the picture today, I recognize most of these heroic men.

Mr. Walters, whose father, a Union soldier under General

Sherman was wounded and died in Andersonville Prison, had been asked to write an appropriate poem for the occasion. Its title was *"To The Veterans Of The Blue And The Gray."* It is almost impossible to read it, as well as the short articles the widows wrote in the booklet, without shedding a few tears.

This, my fellow citizens, is the true story of our Civil War Cannon which stands in our own Courthouse Yard after being dedicated on October 1, 1910.

Barton County Civil War Veterans
(Front to Rear)

Left Side: (Union)	*Right Side: (Confederate)*
John McInterfer	Ed G. Ward
Dr. W. L. Griffin	Gordon Pointer
James Hall	K. D. Griffin
Mack Neese	G.A. Bandy
Alan Cockrell	J.W. Short
Lafe Lisher	M. Stemmons
Mike McKee (far left)	

"More Yesterday In Barton County"

May 13, 1981

In Genevieve Guinn's article of May 7 on "Yesterday in Barton County," she posed several questions, one of which I can clear up for her and for others who are interested.

First, however, I want to point out that there is some questions as to whether Allen Petty and his wife Ellinor were the first white settlers here or whether it was buckskin clad Jesse Kelley who settled just west of the present Highway 71 on Boston road. Several of us attended the sale a few years ago, shortly after the last Kelley sister died. All these years this farm had remained in the hands of old Jesse's descendants. I have read that he arrived about 1820 and became very friendly with the Osage Indians nearby.

Some say the Pettys arrived about 1830 and first lived a few miles out of the present Lamar. By the way, Pettis Creek is named for the Pettys with a slight name change. We'll never know for sure which family arrived first, though it doesn't really matter.

As for the Pettys living in several different counties, yet never changing their location, the following is the explanation of that, Genevieve.

Missouri became a state on August 10, 1821. Previous to that it was known as Missouri Territory. When we achieved statehood of Southwest Missouri was placed in Wayne County. Then in 1833 Green County was carved out of Wayne and Springfield was made the county seat. We were then a part of Green County.

In 1844 Jasper county was formed out of Green and Carthage was designated the county seat of this new county. So now Mr. Petty was living in Jasper County through he wouldn't be very long. Lastly, through the efforts of our first college educated settler, George E. Ward, the northern part of Jasper county in 1855 became Barton County. It was named for David Barton who Was Missouri's first Constitutional Convention president in 1821. He later became one of the first two United States Senators from the new state. The other one was David Hart Benton.

Another Interesting side light concerns the first political squabble in the county. This was over the location of the county seat. Those out east wanted it somewhere on Horse Creek and those in the west part thought it should be somewhere on the ridge west of the village of Lamar. Later, those in the eastern part, particularly around Milford and vicinity, switched and wanted it in Golden City.

To settle the argument, the governor appointed a committee of three from nearby counties to make the decision. One requirement was that 50 acres of land had to be deeded to the county. So Mr. Ward paid his son-in-law Joseph Parry $5. per acre for 40 acres and Elisha Peters $15. per acre for 10, making a total of 50 acres. While Mr. Ward paid for the acreage, he allowed the sellers to deed their land to the county. As a result the committee decided Lamar should be the county seat.

More On Yesterday In Barton County

June 9, 1981

On May 18, the eyes of our nation were turned toward the Old Post Office at Notch, Missouri, in the Ozarks where Levi Morrill, better known as Uncle Ike, held forth for many years.

The Postmaster General of the United States and other dignitaries were present that day to participate in the ceremony, since it was the occasion for placing on sale the new 18-cent "Surrey With The Fringe On Top" stamp rolls, known as coils in Post Office lingo.

What more appropriate time could there be to reveal some startling information about Uncle Ike and his family and their former connection with Lamar?

I am indebted to the Leroy Erwins for allowing me to read this booklet, "The Story Of Uncle Ike and the Shepherd of The Hills Characters," written by son Oscar, and also to Tom Steeper for telling me about the booklet in the first place.

The Erwins were visiting the old post office several years ago and when the son learned they were from Lamar, he especially wanted them to have one of his booklets.

I doubt if many know that Levi Morrill, who later was to famous as Uncle Ike, moved to Lamar from Marmaton, Kansas, in 1875 and published a newspaper called "The Lamar Advocate." On December 12, 1880, he married a Miss Jennie Dickerson. Truman Powell, an associate in operating the newspaper, and who was also a Justice of the Peace, performed the ceremony.

The son, Oscar was born here in 1881 and on January 23, 1884, a little girl, Susie B. was delivered by Dr. Dye.

All this was such surprising information, that I went to the courthouse and had a copy made of the marriage record, as well as that of Susie's birth. Since our county clerk's office has no birth records for 1881 or before, I was unable to get one of Oscar's birth.

While living here, Levi went on a hunting trip with friends to the Ozarks. He was so taken with the beauty there that he came home, sold his interest in the paper to Powell and after living here 18 years, moved his family in three wagons to the Ozarks, where they all spent the rest of their lives.

Many know that Levi Morrill was Uncle Ike in Harold Bell Wright's book, "*Shepherd of the Hills.*" But, do we know that Sammy Lane was actually Susie Morrill? Most of the book's characters were people who lived nearby and who came to Uncle Ike's Post Office for their mail and to "sit a spell" and visit.

June 21, 1981 Uncle Ikes Post Office In the Ozarks, Notch, Missouri

Shepherd Of The Hills Cemetery, Notch, Missouri.

Uncle Ikes Of The Novel By Harold Bell Wright "Shepherd Of The Hills."

Because Morrill was the oldest postmaster in the United States, he was called to Kansas City by the chamber of commerce to dedicate the first air mail service between Kansas City and St. Louis, Missouri.

For christening the plane, he used a bottle of water taken from his home.

He never fully recovered from the tiring trip, and died three months later on August 22, 1926, the day after his 89th birthday.

Both he and his daughter Susie (Sammy Lane), who died in 1916, are buried in the Shepherd of the Hill Cemetery, formerly known as the Evergreen Cemetery. It is only about one mile from the Old Post Office.

In the last chapter of the booklet, son Oscar describes the restful, peaceful beauty of the Ozarks and speaks glowingly of what it has meant to him to live his life out there. He closed by saying "I have lived here since 1893 when we moved here from Lamar."

The Joplin Globe, Sunday, October 25, 1981.

Ozark Hall Of Fame Welcomes Inductees Today

Levi Morrill (1837-1926), gained lasting recognition as a model for character in the novel "***The Shepherd of the Hills.***" Born in Portland, Main, he studied law and graduated from Bowdoin College in 1852, a contemporary of Longfellow and Hawthorne.

As a protege of Horace Greeley at the New York Tribune, Morrill followed his mentor's advice in the mid-1880s and went West -- to Kansas, where he worked on and later founded and published numerous newspapers.

He served in the seventh Kansas Calvary during the Battle of Shiloh and after the war he followed his newspaper profession, practiced law and established a newspaper at Lamar.

In 1893, with $1.25 in his pocket, he moved to the Ozarks to a 160-acre farm in Stone County. That homestead, together with the Levi Morrill Post Office at Notch, has been preserved by members of the Morrill family and is listed in the National Register of Historic Places.

During his years as postmaster, Levi Morrill befriended a fellow Easterner, Harold Bell Wright, when Wright first visited the Ozarks in 1895. There friendship eventually was highlighted by Wright's inclusion of Levi (Uncle Ike) and his post office in ***"The Shepherd of the Hills."*** Morrill was recognized and honored as the nation's oldest living postmaster shortly before his death in August 1926, at the age of 89.

What Independence Day Means To Me

July 3, 1981

When Opal Sims called yesterday and asked me to do this article for tonight's paper, my first thought was that I just couldn't do it on such short notice. Then, as we talked, ideas began flashing into my mind. The following are my thoughts on what it actually does mean to me.

Nationally, it came to my mind first that this is the 205th birthday of our Nation. A glorious declaration of liberation from tyranny and despotism came into being on July 4, 1776.

I thought of how I fought back the tears when I visited Thomas Jefferson's grave near his home, Monticello. I realized full well what a struggle he and the founding fathers had gone through to assure us that we are endowed by our Creator with certain inalienable rights, as life, liberty and the pursuit of happiness.

Perhaps on this day, we should admit that too many of us are confusing liberty with license. The freedom we have is not simply freedom to do as we please, but to do what is right. One, so many of us ignore, is the right to vote. Think for a moment how few people in the world have this privilege. We could lose it, you know.

We must constantly guard against the erosion of our freedoms. No longer can we take them for granted because unseen forces are working to take them from us.

This is the time to take stock of ourselves as to whether we are accepting the responsibilities that go along with our heritage of independence and if we are truly thankful that we are citizens of this great country. To me, this is also a time of rejoicing and expressing our patriotism. It is certainly regrettable that we have lost so much of our patriotic fervor.

Thinking of the Fourth brings back many happy memories of celebrations as I was growing up. There was the time when we started into town in our surrey with the fringe on top almost before dawn. We wanted to arrive early so we wouldn't miss a single event of the big day on the square. What fun it was to watch the sack races, the three-legged races, the efforts of the men and boys to catch the greased pig and to see and hear the firecrackers exploding all around us.

We four girls were always given a nickel each to spend after eating our lunch of crackers, bologna and cheese on the Courthouse lawn. What a time we had deciding whether to buy an ice cream cone or glass of pink lemonade.

The patriotic speeches in the afternoon and the display of fireworks after dark ended a happy and exciting day. These brilliant displays continued until July 4, 1928 when all the fireworks on the truck, which had been pulled to the northwest corner of the square, caught fire and exploded with a violent outburst, sending people scurrying in every direction!

This day also brings memories of the three Boss boys tossing gravel up to our bedroom window before dawn to awaken us girls, so we could dress and slip out (or so we thought) to start shooting our private purchases.

Neither can I think of July 4th without calling to mind the many family gatherings when we always had fried chicken, home made ice cream and lemonade.

Then there is the vivid memory of the thrill felt when I first viewed that great lady standing in New York City Harbor. She is the symbol of justice and freedom for those of us who call America home. Let us never forget that!

Recalling Some Fair History

August 19, 1981

Now that our annual Fall Festival is fast approaching, it seems an appropriate time to recall a bit of its past history.

Many of our people do not realize there was a County Fair long before the free fairs now being held on the public square.

According to historical records, the very first one was held in 1872, yes 1872, under the auspices of the Barton County Agricultural and Mechanical Society, with 100 members. They purchased 35 acres at the northwest edge of Lamar near Muddy Creek. The Vo-Tech school is now located on the east part of this land. The first officials were Charles G. VanPelt, president; S.C. Avery, vice president; R.B. Robinson, secretary and Allen Cockrell the man who bought the Civil War cannon for us, as treasurer. There were 9 directors on the original board, one of whom was Joe Parry, son-in-law of George E. Ward, one of Lamar's founders.

The fair was a big event in the lives of our citizens. It usually lasted four days and was always held in either August or September.

I can still see in my mind's eye, the many white buildings on the grounds, some large and some not so large. These were used for various exhibits. Then there were horse stables, the house where the caretaker lived and the big grandstand where we could sit in the shade and watch the races, rest a bit or see and hear the special entertainment. Also, there were stands here and there selling food and drinks. The pink lemonade always took my eye as a child.

Then there was dust and dust and more dust! I can still see Ben Lucas driving the two white horses hitched to the water wagon as he drove around the race track settling the dust before the races were to start.

The horse races were the big attraction of each afternoon. How well I remember, Kenneth, better known as Pat Griffin, as he mingled in the crowd selling the racing programs for 10 cents each.

In later years, we also had car races and how exciting they were! A mechanic always went with the driver. He usually stood on the running board and swayed outward on the curves to prevent the car from turning over. Tragedy struck in 1917, however, when Hugh Long had his mechanic, George Rains, a brother of Opal Walters, crashed into a maple tree and the board fence. Hugh was killed instantly, but George escaped with only a broken leg. Charles Hylton and Calvin Nowlin had climbed up into this same tree to watch the races and narrowly escaped serious injury.

According to E.J. Mann, Willard Walters, a rural mail carrier and grandfather of Allen, took his annual vacation at fair time. He served as the Marshall, riding around the grounds on a beautiful palomino mare, which he borrowed each year from Jesse Mann.

I shall always remember the year Blind Boone, the famous Negro pianist, held all of us in the grandstand, spellbound with his renditions of the popular songs.

Then there was the time a hot-air-filled balloon was sent aloft filling the gaping audience with wonder. How it was filled is a story in itself. And who could ever forget the first time a "flying machine" landed and took the daredevils up for a circle over town for just a few cents?

Many walked to the grounds, but if you had the money, you could ride in a jitney from the square to the gate for 10 cents, so says Elza D. Smith, 1405 Broadway.

Others came in carts, buggies, surreys, wagons and even on horseback. A special place was provided near the north gate for these vehicles and the horses. So people coming this way entered at the north gate. In later years, they came in Model T's, Flanders, Reos, Packards or Stanley Steamers if they had the money to buy these new-fangled contraptions.

The fair gradually became a money loser. Some think the Crawford Comedians, who put on their delightful show each evening in a tent erected where Memorial Hall now is (according to several old timers), were the culprits. People rushed home early, if they had gone at all, to get the chores done, so they could get back in early to attend this favorite of all shows.

Others say it was because the grounds were so often flooded. Who could ever forget that big flood of September 16, 1915?

I have not been able to determine the exact year the gates were closed for good. I know it was after 1925, for I have here a fair booklet of that year which belongs to Frank Fast.

There was no fair for several years. However, sometime near 1932, Earl Williams and Paul Brown with a few other enterprising business men promoted a sort of mini-fair on the square. A small carnival set up and along with this, there was the animal judging on the east side. According to George Leker, in those earliest years, the stock was brought in, judged and then taken home. Edith Klein says the exhibits like we have today in Memorial Hall were displayed and judged in the building now occupied by Roberts Store and Horton's Variety Store. This space was all one then. It had housed Steelman's Restaurant, but was vacant just then.

A few years later, community-minded Bud Moore got into the act and as many of us know, served as the manager until his death in 1968. Now, his two sons are carrying on what their father had so ably developed into one of the state's largest free fairs. We do indeed, owe Bud a great debt of gratitude, for without him, we might not now have this great fall event which I, among many others enjoy to the hilt.

The Flood At The Fairgrounds, 1915. Bill Bummett With his horse and spring wagon. Flooding may have been reason for Fair on square.

School In Review

October 7th and 8th, 1981

Since our high school sent forth it's first graduated class 100 years ago this coming spring, it seems an appropriate time to take a look at the development of our county educational system.

Old records indicate that the very first school was held in a crude log cabin about two miles south of Lamar. The year was 1854 and William Seals was the teacher.

The second one we know about was held in a vacant house in what then was the west part of town. A. R. Randall taught this school.

It is believed the first regular school building erected here was a little frame structure about a block from the public square. It was built in 1866 and abandoned in 1871. For several years it was occupied by various families, including Johnny Metsinger and his mother.

I feel certain this little school house is now the kitchen of Edith Klein's home. Joseph Parry, who was very prominent in early day affairs lived, at that time, in the white frame house next door south. It still stands there today.

In the meantime, log school houses were appearing here and there in the timber. They had little or no equipment and usually were near small settlements. Before that, children were taught in various homes.

Up to the close of the Civil War most of the teachers were men. By 1870 many of the buildings had been replaced by frame, brick or stone ones, and a few women were being hired.

One of our very early schools was in the vicinity of what is now Howell Cemetery, south of Milford. It was called the Owens school. I have a couple of books used by my grandparents, Dora Tharp and Jim Lee, when they attended this school in the early 1870's.

As the population in the county grew, townships were formed. There was an attempt to have a school in each one. How well I remember these dotted over the county, something like 100 in all. I recall, too, how sad many of us felt when it was finally voted to close those still operating and consolidate, as they called it. Some of the children went to Golden City, others to Liberal and the majority entered the Lamar Schools.

My own very first exposure to a formal education was at Prairie Rose between here and Milford. What a thrill to ride to school in the buggy with the Alf Whitaker "kids"! It was during this year that my three little sisters found my beautiful doll, which I thought I had well hidden, and punched in her eye.

A year at Milford after our farm home burned and another year or so at Cherry Grove with Matie Rudisale, now Veale, as our much beloved teacher, ended my attendance in rural schools.

However, later I was destined to spend two happy years as a country teacher. One was at Oakton another at Doylesport. To this day, I am in touch with many of my former pupils.

According to the Lamar Republican's historical supplement published in 1905, the Lamar School District was organized in December 1870. The first under the new system opened January 2, 1871 with only three teachers. The head teacher's office was in the Baptist church which was the only one here at that time. The other two rooms were in a frame building near where Mr. Johnson's livery stable was. Anyone know just where that was?

The supplement also said that Golden City organized soon after we did and was followed shortly by Liberal, Iantha and Minden Mines.

At one time there were three ward schools here besides the Washington building which served all grades through high school. The Franklin was at 11th and Truman across the street south of the Truman birthplace. Wray was on the northeast corner of 9th and Jefferson and Logan was on the southeast corner or 12th (now highway 160) and Walnut. So far as I can learn these last three only had classes through the fourth grade.

Eventually the ward schools were closed and all children went to Washington. By the way, the original Washington had burned in the late 1880's and was replaced with a very up to date building which was later called Central.

When I entered the fifth grade in 1912 I went to Central. I might add that it was quite a thrill to be going to such a big school.

Reba Griffin, now Streeper, and I decided that year we would each write a novel. Each morning we met at the south steps and read to each other what we had written. I wonder what ever became of those novels?

We also had a small school for the Negro children living here then. It still stands at the southwest corner of 14th and grand and for many years has been the home of the late Polar Bear (Jesse) Swift and his wife.

We even had a college for awhile! An ad in one of the 1897 issues of the Southwest Republican stated that it was to open September 15th. Old timers recall it was at the east end of what is now 17th street. It was College back then.

When I was a teenager, one of the "in" things to do was to walk on Sunday afternoons, out beautiful tree lined college street to this imposing brick structure. Our old "Kodak" books hold many pictures taken on these afternoons.

It later was a Catholic school, but that did not do too well, either. Mr. Josh Box finally bought the building and much of the brick was used in Memorial Hall.

A need was felt for a new grade school. According to Ted Windes, former superintendent, this was started in 1954, through it wasn't ready for occupancy until a year or so later.

In 1962 Old Central was torn down and the new building, the present high school, was built. Mabel de Lissa says that May of 1963 was a red letter month for then they started moving into rooms as they were completed.

On May 7, 1963, the people voted bonds for junior high addition.

In September 1972, the vo-tech school was opened to serve an extensive area, eight schools in all, in a much needed field.

I for one, am very proud of the educational facilities here in Lamar, as well as in Liberal and Golden City. I find myself wishing I could have had more of the advantages you young people have here today.

What do you suppose William Seals would think if he could know of all these changes and see the well equipped building we have in Barton County now? They are indeed a far cry from his crude one room log cabin.

The first High School-"The Washington" was built in 1871-1872. It burned in the mid 1880's and on 1894 the next High School of buff brick and marble was erected. This last one was called Washington School for a few years. But when the Ward Schools, Wray, Franklin and Logan closed all children then went there. So it became Central School with grades on the first floor and the High School upstairs.

Lamar High School

Old Negro School

Old Nicknames

January 19, 1982

Do people living here now nickname their friends as they did in earlier days?

While recovering recently from an arm fracture, I had plenty of time to ponder on this. With the assistance of family members and a few friends, I listed ones we could recall. In a very short time, I had close to 100 and I'm sure there are many, many more.

The reasons for some is obvious. For instance, old timers remember that Wallace Griffin was called Heavy, which was a direct contrast to his small build. Alfred Klein grew up in his grandfather Barth's home. Mr. Barth was a Tin Smith, so Alfred soon was called Tinner. We can assume that Ralph Diamond is Dockery because his father was a dentist. Earl Turner early got the name Happy, for he was always singing, whistling and acting happy.

Then there are many others that can't be explained so easily. However, we do know there is a story behind each nickname. For instance, why is Bob Woodward called Toad, and his brother, Carl, Clutch? Another puzzle is Cecil Kazee's name Hedge. I had to call Margaret Bickel to ask what Spike's real name is. I've never heard any thing but Spike. Anyone know why Charles Young was called Peck in his earlier days?

Ever wonder why Clarence Arnold is Yippie and where Wallace Earp picked up the name Skeet? And how come everyone called Lloyd Quick, Beans? Suppose beans were his favorite food? Also try to explain this one - Smoke Bucket Willis.

Many of you know Stew Fry, but have you heard he is really Emery? And who in the world is Harry Thiebaud? Bet you don't know Lucky Robert's real name either. Do you know that Bub Curless isn't really Bub at all?

Many remember Claude Whitchurch as Cotton, Jess Swift as Polar Bear, Harold Boss as Bowser and Gates Armstrong as Doc.

When I taught Floyd Boles at old Doylesport school, he wasn't yet Smokey. That name came later and stayed with him all his life.

Another of my students there was Forest Waits. I can still see and hear him coming across the field to school and always singing, "Anyone Here See Kelly?" Thus he became Kelly and it stuck.

Then there is Cack Neale, Shorty Smith, Dago Fast, Chick Satterlee, Hook Dermott, Dutch Smith, Brother Adams and Jap Combs. Do you know their real names?

I once knew Dink Rice, Shovel Moore, Cuddy VanPelt, Hank

Horton, Granger Twist Rains, Gilly Guilfoyle, Brother Jones, Chicky Faubion, Tickle Turner, Spon Lee, Big Boy McMurphy, Rip Collins, Punk Niehaus, Huckle Berry Berry, Pickle Glaze, Diddy Duncan, Goon Snip, Casey Castle, Cap Joyce, Bud Moore, Boy Wright, Big and Ugly Harrington and Three Finger Johnson.

No one now knows why Claude Yates was always called Toodle Bug, or how come cute little Dean Baker early got the name Cannon Ball, or where Ross White got the name Rooster. Here's the best one yet - Ocean Toad Fast was none other than Dan, a brother of Dago. I mean Frank!

It seems more men than women here have been given nicknames. Why, I don't know. But, do you know the real name of these local women. . . Pug Thieman, Reenie Collins, Toots Streeper, Boo Wirts, Shorty Godfrey, Tootie McCluey, Nonnie Stahl, Putter Perry, Sis Martin and Spanky Robinson?

Is this a habit of small towns and rural communities only? Personally, I believe it is something to cherish, for it denotes a closeness and a friendliness not found in cities.

More Nicknames

February 3, 1982

I had no idea may article on nicknames would be of so much interest. In fact, I was somewhat dubious about writing it and did delay for some time.

So many of you called expressing your enjoyment and appreciation. Some gave me more names and asked me to do a second article.

And so, article two using as many more nicknames as possible follows, because "you asked for it!"

Again, the reason for some is quite clear. Clarence Chiles, a former mortician here, was called Digger for obvious reasons. Remember how tall Earl Rutherford, a former mayor, was? That explains why he was known to everyone as Slim. Do you recall Meredith Daubin, the youngest brother of Admiral Freeland Daubin of World War II fame? He was called Little Crit after his father, Crittenden. George Boss was Two-Step, due to a limp which followed a childhood paralysis.

I often think of other old timers who were never called by their real name. There was the prominent businessman, T.W. Harkless, who was Toss to everyone, Curley Hosselton Sr., a hotel and rooming house operator was never called Anis, his legal name.

Then there was Leonard Knight, a clerk in the Harkless store, who went by Mugsy and Leon Jewell who was known as Jelly. Who could ever forget Peanut Wilson and his polite ways? Know his real name? Remember Midnight Williams, so called because of his night walking?

I can still see the two Clark brothers going home from town. We called them Friday and Saturday because the tall one, Friday, always walked in front of Saturday, the short one. Their real names have escaped me.

Why was Edgar Bloomfield called Sticker, Earl Blair, Toots and Clarence Werts, Chick? Two men once lived here who had the name George Cox. One was called Long George and the other Hog George. Remember them?

Who could ever forget those high flying Koehler boys, George and Clarence, who dazzled all the girls with their big shinny cars? I never learned why Clarence was called Skunch.

Remember Cussin' Griff? Would you believe his real name was Melville Griffith? Gravy Gibson was another one. It took several telephone calls to learn he was Archie.

Wonder if you know the real names of the following - Chigger Earp, Punky Logue, Bogus Bartlett, Hoopity Feezel, Pole Hoss Johnson, Slats Donalson, Yick-a-poo Johnson, Ching-a-long Rogers, Katz Schubert, Turner Clark, Punk Thompson, T Dub Streeper, Pole Elam, Wobbit Payne, Ebutter Cassidy and Cutter Venable?

Wouldn't you like to know why Floyd Wirts is Frog, Jules DeMaire is Hoolio, Leonard McCoy is Nig, Wilmer Hagins is Cotton and why Leon Couch was known as Mickey? By the way, I understand there is sometimes an Isadore DeMaire. Is it Roy, or is it Jules?

Oh yes, Goon Snip was not Bob as you likely thought. His real name was Warren Neal. How about that - two nicknames.

Do you know the name Pat Griffin's parents gave him? It sure wasn't Pat! And what is Snort Rose's actual name? Another Thiebaud puzzler is Cobb. Now who is that?

See if you can identify each of these women by their legal name - Al Griffin, Buddy Snorgrass, Sickie Moore, Jimmie Finley, Kinky Thiebaud, Myrt Sherron, Boo Reed, Dode Miller, Snippy Combs, and Sunshine Tipton.

The way of all these nicknames may never be known. But, isn't it fun to recall them?

Still More Nicknames
March 1, 1982

The continuing interest in local nicknames is almost unbelievable! Hardly a day passes that someone doesn't call to give me a name or two, or just to talk about his or her interest in the other two articles. Would you believe that nearly 100 more names have come my way? Tom Snead sent me quite a list. Others have come by mail and also some have been left at the house when we have been away.

I even had a call from Washington D.C. No, it wasn't President Reagan calling! It was our friend of many years, Meredith Daubin who wanted to tell us that it was Toss Harkless who gave him the nickname, Little Crit, when he was just 8 years old.

He also said that Arthur Aull, our long time Democrat editor and publisher, was actually responsible for many of our nicknames. He would write up an event in his usual colorful way and very likely use an expression which would lead to one. For instance, in writing an account of a game he had seen, he said, "The ball that Dean Baker threw literally flew across the field like a cannon ball." That was all the kids needed and Dean was Cannon Ball Baker the rest of his life.

So many of you have asked me Spike Bickel's real name, that I think I'd better ease your minds. It is Carl!

How could I ever have left our Pat Gibbs in the previous articles when I have known him all his life? If you have been thinking that is his real name, you are wrong.

And then, there was that dear little 5th grader at Oakton School, Waldemar Schlipp. The very first day I wore my diamond engagement ring to school, he asked me what it meant. I doubt if many here now remember him as Waldemar, for he has been Dutch for many years.

No wonder N.B. Elam used initials instead of writing our his full name when the teacher requested it! Can you feature parents giving a child the name of Napoleon Bonaparte?

A good many years back there was a school superintendent here whom the kids called Marble Top Nichols because he had so little hair. I doubt if he ever knew this.

Have your ever wondered about the actual name of these men who once lived here--Josh Box, Fielder Jones, Chinless McClanahan, Doc Rice, Bud Dale, Colonel Selvey, Spin Isenhower, Bub Rix, Jr., Lum Chancellor, Preach Haddock, Shorty Cox, Dock Selvey and Dick Walter? No, that last one is not a mistake.

I can understand why Gordon Boyer is called Councilor but how come Gerry Miller is Grease, Jim O'Neal is Biggie, Carl Moore is Cedar and Ramon Hyett is Jacko? And Where did Eddie Gould get the name Rat and Jack Isenhower that of Hard Rock? Bet these are interesting stories.

Do you remember that Wallace Konantz was Scrappy when he lived here--or was it Harold? I always thought Barney Brummett was really Barney and then I learned recently he is Ralph Shucks!

Even L.D. Porter once had a nickname, though he may not have been aware of it. My uncle Reed Boles always called him Pound-a-Porter.

Then there are other queer names -- each with a story, I'm sure. Here are a few--Pinkie Rogers, Red Dalton, Buzzy Gardner, Blind Parker, Digger Buzzard, Shorty Webb, Lefty Boles, Monkey Ward, Longun Workman, Donald Duck Overton, Toad Basset, Runt Stahl, Buck Mason, Bud Hicks, Skinny Guilfoyle, Short Alumbaugh, Dutch Godfrey, Shorty Lawless, Bus Meredith, Left Fast, Bud Sumners, Tickle Boyd, Acey Talbott and Duck Daetwyler.

As usual, I have only a few names for the gals. Know these? Shorty Lincoln, Totts Morin, Smitty Lee, Dumplin Moore and Lee Kreeger.

Have you figured out yet why we have always been such a nicknaming community? Maybe this friendliness is what sets us apart as a very special and desirable community in which to live. I've often heard it said that once you have lived in Barton County, you'll eventually return. I'm inclined to believe it. We did!

Should Have Thought Of Those Nicknames

April 29, 1982

Recently, a long time friend, Ted Hackney brought me a list of nicknames I should have thought of before this. Many are people who lived here some time ago,

Imagine forgetting that Toddle Bug Yates had a brother who was called Sing-a-low! A cousin of theirs was Tubby Barger whose sister married Walter J. Miller, the banker's son. Walter's nickname was Youth's Companion, for he could usually be seen after school with his open car piled full of high school kids.

How could I have forgotten the teacher, Corky Foster who married pretty Reba Carlton? We students really thought he had a cork leg. Remember a later teacher Mr. Weiser? You guessed it. His nickname was Bud.

Then there were the Bury Brothers - Toots and Snowd whom everyone knew. Alva Thompson, the baker, was always called Fat. Hickory Akers' legal name was Everett, but who ever used it? Oswald Bishop thought you meant someone else unless you said Newt.

If you ever knew Lynn Finks, you know why he went by the name of Slicky. But why was Don Eddlemon called Dizz and Clyde Sellers Peck?

When we moved to Lamar, I heard people speak of Bill Moore. It was some time before I learned they meant Ralph. I hear his son goes by Winky. I wonder why?

No one ever called Arthur Egbert anything but Cap. Remember his relative Lawrence Anderson whom we all nicknamed Red? What a loveable character he was!

Then there was Abe Crosswhite, Monk Mann, Crip Coiner, Bugger Stansbro (uncle of Otis), Bus Vaughn, Beans Dickerson, Bally Isenhower, Biddy Batesman, Colonel Slinker, Dusty Rhodes, Bid Cole and Hank O'Rear.

I understand there were two Divines here once Nub and Coony. I don't believe they were related.

No one could ever forget Spankly Russel Ray, whom we schoolmates named Busty, nor good looking Donald Cobb who was always called Ty. Know who Baby Face Shepherd was? He was Harold, an uncle of Margaret Couch and Betty Kentner.

Someotherswere Tally (Frank) Ehret, Tink (Lynn) York, Ted (Chester) Weidman and that sporty Neil McAdow who answered to the name of Sport. What else?

Now why was mild mannered Lester Evilsizer called Pistol Pete? Bet that is an interesting story. Wayne Pierce was Preach. That's easy to figure, as his father was the Baptist pastor.

If we needed transportation we could always hire Hy-Power Oehring. He had a liking for high powered cars and used them for his jitney service.

Who could ever forget Hurt and Bonney's North Side Bakery? I've never figured out why Claude Hurt was known as Johnny Bull. It didn't seem to fit?

Know who Laughin' Reiley was? Remember Hack Tyler, Bud and Babe Guilfoyle, Bugs Little, Dutch Hatfield and the Neihaus fellows -- Hoot (Clayton) and his uncle Bing who was actually William?

Jack but I understand he was Howard.

Which one of the DeMaires is called Frog by many of his friends? Irkle knows.

Sis Martin says her son Gene's nickname is Nero. Does that fit him? I'm sure you have heard of Dobbin' Ford, but do you know he is actually John? Surely everyone ate at Cooky's in Golden City when Cecil Ambler ran it. How many of you ever called him Cecil, though?

Ted came up with just two nicknames for the ladies. Know who Speck Hoover is? I dare say you don't know that Betty Shelton isn't really Betty. What is her real name?

I can't close without asking you old timers if you have heard of the fiddler's contest held here in Lamar on October 22, 1914? According to a son now living in Jasper, Charley Andrews, down near Coon Creek, won and Arthur Aull named him "the Fiddlin' Tornado of Coon Creek." His prize was a $10 gold piece and a real leather suitcase. Eventually he was champion of Missouri, Kansas, Arkansas and Oklahoma. That name stayed with him all his life, by the way.

I honestly believe Barton County could win a contest for using the most nicknames of any community. There seems to be no end, but please folks, no more!

Life Was Less Complex Then

April 1, 1982

Growing up in the early 1900's here in Barton County was far from what it is today! Life was much less complicated and we lived at a much slower pace. We had no high powered cars, no radios, no televisions, no super markets, no mechanized farm equipment and only a few people had electric lights and indoor bathrooms.

Back then, our chief mode of transportation was either horseback or in horse-drawn vehicles, such as buggies, surreys, spring wagons and the old farm wagon.

There was no getting places in a few minutes as we do today. I recall one time when my Aunt Emma Lee (Boles) and I made a trip in a buggy from Nashville to Milford. We left at dawn and arrived at my great-grandmother Howell's after dark. We forgot how weary we were when she sat us down to a supper of fried country cured ham, red eye gravy, biscuits and honey.

Going places in winter was a different story. Bricks were heated, wrapped and put at our feet to help keep us warm. I can still see that heavy black lap robe which we tucked about us to keep the winter cold out. Even then, we nearly froze.

Can you imagine how excited people were when the first cars appeared on Lamar streets? Some declared they were the work of the devil and would never survive.

I remember when my Uncle Sam Lee bought his first one. . . a single-seated doorless roadster. We four sisters thought we were in hog heaven when he took two of us at a time around the block in that wonderful new horseless contraption. We felt as though we were almost flying!

Meals were prepared on the old iron cook stove and what other heat we had came from the stove in the front room--usually a Round Oak heater.

We children didn't get up mornings until after the grate had been shook down, as we expressed it then. When we thought the stove was red hot, we would grab our long underwear, our black sateen bloomers, our petticoats and the other garments children wore then and make a dash for the stove. Our clothes went on in a flash, but getting the legs of that long underwear folded over so we didn't have too big a lump at our shoe tops were quite a chore.

You have missed something if you have never slept on a straw "tick" topped with a feather bed, which was so soft you almost disappeared. Remember all those heavy wool comforters under which you could scarcely move?

Most of us went all the way through school doing our evening studying by the light of a coal oil lamp. I wonder now how we ever

-25-

did our lessons with such poor lighting.

What a joy to come home from school and smell fresh baked light bread in the kitchen! Usually, we were each given a thick warm slice and out to the garden we'd go in the spring for green onions or a radish. These were washed at the well in the back yard for there was no running water in the house those days. I think I shall never taste anything more delicious.

Springtime always meant trips out into the fence rows, pastures and timber to gather greens. It was an education for the children who went along, as they learned quickly which weeds were not to be picked. How good greens smelled simmering in the old iron pot with saltpork or bacon for seasoning! Along with green onions, navy beans and corn bread, we had a meal fit for a king, as we always said.

Have you ever churned butter? Our arms got tired moving that dasher up and down, but we forgot that when we spread that fresh butter on our bread. Remember how we cooled the buttermilk by lowering a pail into the well for several hours? Ice boxes came along later, you know.

We didn't have radios, televisions or stereos, but we did have gramaphones, later phonographs and still later victrolas. Our first gramaphone with its big red horn and cylinder records was purchased in the spring of 1908. Then on August 8 our farm home burned to the ground. I remember screaming for my mother to get it and my new straw hat, but she got neither one.

I do believe we four girls and the two Griffin children, Reba and Kenneth, had the very first "wireless" in Lamar. We lived close enough that we could attach a can at both ends of a long string running from each back yard. Every morning and evening we "talked" to each other via string and tin can wireless. What fun!

How would you like to have asafetida tied in a small piece of cloth and hung around your neck all winter to keep the germs away? I can still smell the "stinking stuff" when I think about it. Don't you know the school rooms had a foul odor all winter?

There were social activities a plenty then-or so we thought. Families sometimes got together for an opossum and sweet potato supper and at other times perhaps a fried rabbit gravy and biscuit meal. These were fun occasions for the children.

Then the grown folks often had either play parties or square dances in the homes. They square danced at both, but there was one big difference! At the ones called square dances, they added "fiddle" music. Only the more daring did this, for that was a sin and definitely frowned upon by the "good" folk of the community.

We children looked forward to the ice cream suppers and the oyster stew meals held during the winters. We knew we would get to play with other children. I remember an ice cream supper at Milford when I played so long with the Clarence and Maud Werts' kids that I didn't get any ice cream.

Some day, I feel like the old timer who once said, "Jiminy Crickets, hain't life changed since I was a boy?"

Could the next seventy five or so years possibly bring as many changes as some of us have seen?

"We Teenagers Had Fun, Too."

July 29, 1982

If you think being a teenager before 1920 was dull, with nothing to do, you are sadly mistaken. True, we had no radios or televisions and no community swimming pools. Cars were scarce as hen's teeth and we had very little money to spend. We depended on our own initiative and made fun times which didn't require much money.

Sunday School and other church activities played a big part in our lives in those days. Our classes sometimes had parties and how we did enjoy them! I remember one Valentine party when we could ask a boy to go with us. That was my first date. We girls thought we were on top of the world if a boy asked to walk us home after the Sunday evening youth meeting.

Then there was that magic place, Wagner's Bijou, where we spent many a thrill packed evening watching the silent movies, provided we had the nickel for admittance.

As the show started, a picture of a little girl wearing a huge hat was flashed on the screen. The words below said, "Ladies, please remove you hats." The women all wore big hats back then. The little girls pictured was none other then Reba Griffin - now Reba Streeper. Her mother, Mrs. Wallace Griffin was the pianist, for there was no canned or taped music at that time.

I can never forget the Air-Dome run by Sellars and Cribbett for a few seasons. How romantic it was to sit there with your date watching the show with only the stars and sky above.

Many Sunday afternoons, a group of boys and girls would walk out to Lake Cemetery and take pictures. Or maybe we would saunter out tree-line College street - now 17th, to the Old College for more picture taking.

Who could ever forget the many picnics out at the north dam? Little did we dream that place had once been known as ?Roup's Point for an early day settler, Gil Roup, or that it served as a Confederate training camp during the Civil War and was known as Camp Lamar.

Some of the boys were sure to climb atop the old iron bridge and dive into Muddy Creek. I know now that was one way of impressing us girls.

The hay rides, the taffy pulls, the rook parties, the visits to the haunted house, the ice skating parties, the roller skating in the Opera House and the many birthday parties were all such fun. The most daring game we ever played was "post office."

Can you imagine meeting the passenger trains at both depots

being a favorite pastime of us teenagers? We liked to watch the nicely dressed people stepping off or getting on the trains. We couldn't imagine having enough money to ride one. I recall, though, several years later when a second cousin took me by train to Sheldon. What a big deal that was!

During World War I, we always went to see the troop trains going through. Since the trains, with their steam engines, had to take on water, we could talk to the boys who were literally hanging out the windows.

The highlight of every week during the summer was the Saturday night band concert. The townspeople and farmers alike gathered on the square to enjoy this weekly event. It was a great time for the misses to do her grocery shopping and for everyone to catch up on their visiting. Seldom did everything close down before midnight.

We teenagers just existed from one Saturday night to the next. I know we always walked the north and west sides of the square a dozen or more times, hoping the boys would notice us an just perhaps ask to take us home. I believe that was a lot more fun than going around and around in cars as the young people do today.

No Saturday evening ever ended until we visited one of the bakeries for a limeade, a cherry phosphate, a banana split or a sundae. I'll never forget the time some of us ordered nuts on our sundaes and then didn't have enough money to pay the bill. Eddie Casement, an employee of Hurt and Bonney's North Side Bakery trusted us until the first of next week. Not many banana splits were bought for they were 25 cents each.

There wasn't much emphasis on sports in our schools back then. We did have boys' track competition and both boys and girls basketball teams. We had no gym, so practice and played our games at the old Logan grade school. Alberta Snorgrass - now Wirts was a whizz bang player, for she was quick as lighting - well almost!

Our first dates were walking ones. Boys often walked their girlfriends home from school, carrying their books, of course. Ted Hackney tells of the time he walked Marian Rhodes home and loitered too long on the front porch. Her father opened the door and ordered her inside. Ted says he was so scared he ran around the street corner at such speed he gathered sand in his pockets.

As we grew older, Dad sometimes let his son have the horse and buggy and what a thrill it was to ride into the country a few miles.

Later, when people began buying Tin Lizzies (our name for the early Fords) we really felt we were living it up when we had a date with a boy who had his dad's car.

Our parents told us to be home by ten o'clock and that we did, barring unexpected delays. We knew if we didn't we'd be grounded several weeks.

We four sisters were close in ages and so we often dated together. In those days, we preferred being with a group for it was lots more fun.

No article on teenage fun could be closed without mentioning the old porch swing. Many pleasant hours were whiled away swinging and talking as we sipped our cooling lemonade on hot summer evenings with a group of girlfriends or perhaps a date of the evening.

Oh dear, I haven't mentioned our school plays in the old Opera House or other goings on at old Central High. One certain girl in our gang always kept things in an uproar.

Dare you now say, we didn't have fun.

"Our Strange Expressions"

October 7, 1982

Someone has said that in no single phase of life is our reliance on the past more evident than in our day to day language. The cliches and phrases we use give color and also enrich our conversations.

Slang words and expressions tend to come and go. However, some used in the past have managed to survive and are heard yet today.

Do you ever start a sentence with "Was I ever"? If so, you are very likely over 70 years old, for that expression dates back to the late teens and early twenties.

Such phrases as "I'm here to tell you", "the bee's knees", "he's the cat's pajamas", "You're darn tootin", "for crying out loud" and "he's a pain in the neck" are all old slang sayings. So you are giving your age away, if you use them.

As I stated above, some expressions never completely die. Have you ever said "there goes another nail in your coffin"? That dates back to the 18th Century and refers to the smoking habit.

The saying "the jig is up" was popular back in the Elizabethan period. It meant the trick had been exposed, for then, "jig" was slang for trick.

I'm sure you have heard someone say "he's had the wool pulled over his eyes." That goes back to the days when people wore powdered wigs of wool. It evidently started when someone pushed another's wig over his eyes.

Have you ever said "he's not worth a tinker's dam" and then wondered if that was swearing? It wasn't A tinker was a person who mended pots and pans. He made a small dam of clay or bread dough to hold the molten solder while he worked. When he was finished, the dam was worthless and so was discarded. Thus, originated the saying.

I wonder if some of my favorite slang expressions will manage to survive? Quite often, I am asked how I get so much done and my stock reply is "Oh, I just make my shirt tail crack"! If something is crooked, I am apt to say "that's si-goddlen" or, just look how "catty wampus" that is! Just last week, I wanted to clean the kitchen floor and so I told Charles to "Skedaddle", as he was in my way.

Remember when money was "spondulix", a pretty girl was a "peacherina" or a "jazz baby," the head of an organization was "the big cheese," a highly regarded person was "the cat's pajama's," and when we invariable said "Okie-dokie" for just plain yes?

-31-

Just for fun, I've been compiling a list of expressions I have used or heard and in no time at all, I came up with 51. The following are some of them; "You get my goat," "He has bats in his belfry", "He's as busy as a cat eating glue", "Well my monkey's uncle." "Go fly a kite," "She's the cat's me-ow," "He had to eat crow," "That's a pretty kettle of fish," "Hold your horse's," "Go soak your head," "That's a bunch of milarkey," and "More nerve than a Government mule."

Do you think you will live long enough to see someone "laugh his head off," "cry crocodile tears," "give an arm or a leg to anyone," have a cat fit," "shoot off his mouth," or "talk up a storm"?

Occasionally a slang word ends up in Webster's Dictionary. Take the noun "jerk", for instance. It was used for years but not until after 1949 did it appear there. Now it seems due for a long run. Need I tell you it means a stupid, dull or eccentric person?

This isn't the whole "kit and caboodle" by any means, but it is a good place to stop.

"The Name Is The Same"

January 27, 1983

Have you ever thought of the number of names given to both boys and girls? I hadn't until one day Mary Jo Harris named several and said she thought that would make a good topic for an article.

This set me thinking, and in a short while with the help of some others, I had quite a list compiled. I'm quite sure there are many more, however. True, sometimes there is a slight variation in the spelling, though the pronunciation is the same.

The ones mentioned live in our county now, formerly did but now live elsewhere, lived here at one time and are now deceased or are connected with someone here. I may have gone over the county line in an instance or so, but if I did it is because they are well known here.

When a child, I went to school at Milford with Opal Thomas and his sister. It didn't take long to come up with the name of Opal Sims to pair with his. And then I thought of Gene Kentner from down Golden City way and Gene Youngs here in Lamar. Yes, she does spell her name this way.

How about Carol Combs and Carol Leker as well as Gale Wolf and Gayle Shields Day? Most everyone knows Marion Thiebaud, but do you know Marian Roberts, Lucky's wife?

Surely you know or have hard of Terry Moore and Terri Combs Elswick, Cecil Kazee and Cecil Thiebaud, Jerry Moyer and Jerri Curless Finley, Francis Washburn and Frances Ashby, Merle Walker and Merle Sprenkle, Iva Harris and Iva Harry, LaVerne Potter and LaVerne Sprouls, Dean Main and Dean Gariss, Lee Clements and Lee Mallory, Beverly Willhite and Beverly Selvey and then there is my cousin at Milford, Fay Lee. Faye Storm, who is employed by Chastains, came to mind for the lady with that name.

I remember well both Shelby Willey and Shelby Slinker but had never heard of a girl by that name until our grandson and wife at Springfield named their little girl Shelby. So it sometimes is used for both sexes.

Following are some others --- Lou Arft and Lu Rix, Florence Law and Florence Cleveland, Claire Riddle and Claire Wheeler Sutherland, Pearl Wicker and Pearl Faurot, Vivian Costley and Vivian Ambler, June Sharrock and June Julian, Jewell Snip and Jewell Wells, Joe Roe and Jo Thompson, Rubey Ryder and Ruby Weidman, Jess Masterson and Jess Whitchurch, Lynn Castle (Carl's brother -- not daughter) and Lynn Berry Divine, Joy Young and Joy Summers, Leslie Boles and Leslie Harlin, Courtney Roth and Courtney Gilkey, Ray Masterson and Raye Culbertson Carico, Tony Woodward and Toni Thiebaud Cattelino, Ora Faubion and Ora Schultz, Ollie Roberts and Ollie Cross, Gay Sharrock and Gay Payton and lastly, Robin Harrah and Robin Poe.

I thought about Pat Gibbs and Pat Higginbotham. Could these both be nicknames.

Now, had you realized there are even this many? If any man or boy ever comes up to me and says his name is Reba, I'm quite sure I'll fall over in a faint. I can't imagine a baby boy ever being given that name, but who knows!

Just Thinkin'

May 12, 1983

Occasionally, I find a few minutes to think back on events of my earlier days. For one reason or another, some stand out much more clearly than others do.

I have so many fond memories of visiting my great-grandmother Howell, who lived in a story and a half log house just south of Howell Cemetery out Milford way. Yes, they donated the land for the cemetery from their farm.

Perhaps my most vivid memory is the Thanksgiving we were there when the center of the table held a small roasted pig with a red apple in its mouth. That was a strange sight to me and so the picture is still with me as plainly as if it were yesterday.

Never could I forget the day we children decided to go back into the woods after a delicious Sunday dinner at my great Uncle Wes Lee's home.

We hadn't gone far until we ran right into a wolf's den. There was the mother wolf ready to start after us, and several young ones. We almost flew out of the woods, across the field, under the barbed wire fence and back to the house. We were sure that the mother wolf was right behind us!

When I was six, we lived on a farm close to the one where the Kemp Wild West Show had its winter headquarters. Occasionally, some of the Indians would come over and visit with my father, usually bringing a few children along. The headdress of feathers which encircled the head of one of the men and the colorful feathers trailing down his back really fascinated me. We children played peek-a-boo around our fathers' pant legs and chased each other just as children do today. When I tell people I have played, not once, but several times with little Indian children, they look at me as though I must be "off my rocker."

Then there was the day in the early fall of 1912 when Theodore (Teddy) Roosevelt made a whistle stop at the Frisco depot here.

He had formed the Progressive (Bull Moose) party and was opposing the Republican candidate, William H. Taft, for the Presidency. I remember how excited I was to see a national political figure, though I was disappointed because the larger crowd kept me from getting very close.

The night Tom Braniff married Bess Thurman, daughter of Judge Berry Thurman, is another event I like to recall. Little did I dream, as we walked by the home on South Gulf, that lovely summer evening and saw all the bright lights and the people milling around in the yard that this same Tom Braniff would one day become nationally known as the founder of the Braniff Air Lines.

It is also pleasant to think about the nice Negro, Jim Webb, who was the local cab driver meeting all the passenger trains for years and years. Never has a more respected and trusted man lived in Lamar and our mothers always knew he would get us home safely.

How could I ever forget that horrible day, May 28, 1919, when Jay Lynch who had murdered our sheriff John Harlow and his son, Dick, was hanged in a tree on the north side of the courthouse near the entrance. Many of us saw the entire proceedings that day, but when lawman from out of town began asking questions no one saw or knew a thing!

Would you believe we girls dipped our fingers into our moms' flour bin to make the nails white underneath? We just had to have white nails, for that was the style, and how else could we get them?

Or, can you imagine two grade school girls, whom I could name, feeding the grocery delivery boy cold biscuits that the mice had been nibbling on and running over? They had spread jelly on them and he thought they were very good, or so he said.

Oh, there are so many nice memories to recall! And yes, we have plenty of unhappy ones, too, but why dwell on those!

Girls Class Of 1919

June 16, 1983

There can be interesting and exciting life after 80. If you are doubtful, perhaps this article will change your mind, so read on, please.

Five of the six "girls" from this class who live here at the present time get together faithfully on a certain day each month for lunch, laughter and chatter. One of the group, Edith Nall Parson, has a health problem and cannot join us, though she is with us in spirit.

When the employees at Hillcrest Lanes, where we eat, see us coming in they say, "Here comes the over 80 bunch," so we decided to call ourselves the "Over 80 Club."

Not one of us has to depend on a cane or a crutch for support. Instead we trip in, dressed as modishly as you can find anywhere.

Oh, sure, some of us have hearing difficulties and are minus a few parts we brought into the world with us. In spite of broken bones, cataract surgeries and other illnesses, some serious, we are generally speaking in good shape to be over 80. *(You notice I don't say how far past 80.)*

Believe it or not, some of us even have our own teeth yet. A nurse at the hospital not too long ago was dumbfounded when she found I couldn't remove my teeth for her to clean.

Now if you think our conversations at these monthly luncheons center on our health, our operations, our children or our grandchildren, you are wrong again.

We are all interested in world affairs and do keep abreast of the times. We all participate in one way or another in community affairs and our conversation reflects all this.

Usually, someone mentions our younger days. For instance, at our last session, we recalled when Reba Griffin Streeper and Alberta Snorgrass Wirts pleased audiences and especially their current boyfriends, with the rendition of *"When We Come To The End Of A Perfect Day."* I wonder if they could sing it now.

Then one of the "girls" told how hard she tried to put her eye makeup on, so it would resemble Von Wilson Simmons' an upper classmate.

Another one recalled the little black beauty spots we pasted somewhere on our face to give us a sophisticated look, or so we thought. What fun to recall these earlier antics, just so long as it isn't our entire conversation.

Anyone hearing our laughter, our animated voices and topics of conversation, but couldn't see the gray hair most of us have, would never guess us to be over 80. At least, that is what people tell us.

At our class reunion a couple of years ago when celebrated our 62nd anniversary, our esteemed editor came in to take our picture for the paper. His first remark was, "Do you mean there are this many still alive?" Then he was shocked when he heard some had come from California, Florida and Indiana.

I assure you, we aren't letting any grass grow under our feet, nor have any of us taken to the old rocking chair. Would you believe one of our number sees every new show at Branson? Why we might even dance the light fantastic if we were asked.

Irene Goodrum Collins and Maureen Webb Norwood were rather quiet little gals in high school, but I assure you they chatter as much as the rest of us at these monthly luncheons.

Many have commented that it is quite unusual for five old classmates, all over 80 to get together like this. What they really mean is that they are marvelling at the fact we all have our marbles yet and are able to go under our own power.

Anyway, it is fun for we are enjoying life still and finding it quite exciting. We hope we can continue for a long time yet.

Sounds Of Yesteryears

April 24, 1984

Have you ever noticed how much noise we have in our environment today? It came to me rather forcibly recently when the washer and dryer were both running, the stove exhaust fan was on, the teakettle was singing, and on top of all that, the television was on loud enough to drown out the rest. And wouldn't you know, the telephone rang, adding to the noise! All these sounds are in sharp contrast to those prevalent when I was a child.

Back then, we usually were awakened by a rooster crowing somewhere in the neighborhood. In the cold months, we knew we would soon hear someone shaking the grate of the heating stove, and then the rhythmic bang of the bucket on the stove as coal was dumped onto the live coals.

Shortly after this, we heard the coffee beans being ground in the old coffee mill. Who could ever forget the pleasant aroma that permeated the house each morning when this was done? By the way, this was our signal to get out of bed.

We didn't like or enjoy the sound of the dirty clothes being rubbed up and down on the brass wash board though it was a necessary and common one those days. Few people were able to afford the crude electric washers which had come on the market around 1907. Besides not many households had electricity.

A sweeter sound was never heard than when the family gathered around the old pump organ in the evenings to sing their favorite songs. The mother was the one who usually got the job of playing. We children always knew when Ben Lucas was sprinkling the dusty streets with his water wagon, for we could hear the horses and the rumble, rumble of the heavy wagon. How could one ever forget that sound, or for that matter, the similar but quieter one of a horse and buggy coming down the road or street?

Other common sounds then were: hens cackling after laying an egg, cows mooing, horses nickering, the squeak of the lawn or porch swing, our unbuckled galoshes flopping as we walked, someone in the neighborhood chopping wood, a dog barking in the distance, the whistle of the steam engine trains, the church bells tolling, calling us to church, and the teacher's brass hand bell which she always rang to take up school, as we said then.

Everyone had a back yard well with its hand pump which supplied the water for household use. We children were often sent for a bucket of water. Sometimes, we got it too full and spilled it on our legs and shoes which meant, in the winter months, that we

-39-

had same soggy long underwear just above the tops of our shoes.

These are just a few of our everyday sounds when I was growing up. None were harsh or unusually loud and certainly they did not hurt the ears.

Contrast these with those we are accustomed to now. There are the various sirens, power mowers, chain saws, the dish washer, garbage disposal, the electric mixer and the sweeper - to name a few.

Cars and motorcycles make a lot of noise, too. If you don't believe so, listen sometime. Then there are the teenagers who insist upon having their car radios, televisions, record players, going full blast.

We are told that continuous noise over 85 decimals can cause hearing loss. I wonder if we are in danger of having a generation of people with impaired hearing in the near future.

As the old timer said "Hanin't life changed?" I honestly long at time for the quieter sounds of yesteryears.

Our Saturday Night Band Concerts

July 12, 1984

Sometimes I wish television and radio had never been developed for I feel both played a part in the demise of our Saturday night band concerts. These had been held for years in the courthouse yard and were enjoyed by young and old alike.

Ever since I can remember there has been a bandstand in the northwest corner of the large lawn surrounding our stately courthouse. This is where the band presented its weekly concerts during the summers for years and years. The members were local people with fill ins occasionally from Golden City and Liberal.

Gustavus Seyffert, a first cousin of the great German composer Wagner, organized our very first uniformed band in 1889. Other known players at that time were Albert Hays, Charles Parry, O. Hast, E.C. Grant, George Pool and a Mr. Eggars.

By 1915, the players had changed considerably. Albert Hays was now the leader. His son, Harry, also played. And then there was Jud Porter, Earl Holcomb, Reggie Wilson, Arthur Walters, (Uncle of our local photographer, Allen Walters,) and two women, Ocie Elam and Virginia Brigham. I'm sure there were others whom I don't recall.

All old timers remember "Daddy" Owens and his drum, for he never lost an opportunity to lead the parades, Large or small, in the community. I don't believe he ever played in the band, though. The townspeople, as well as the farmers, made it to town on Saturday nights, if possible at all. This was a real social event, anticipated by all, and a time when everyone dressed in their best clothes.

The memory of the teams hitched to all sorts of conveyances and tied to the chain link fence surrounding the courtyard is clearly etched in my mind. By the way, that chain link fence was removed in 1926. No longer any need for it, as cars were now becoming plentiful.

The women did their trading in the grocery stores scattered around the square, before the concert started and left their purchases there until it was time to start homeward. This meant the proprietors had to stay open quite late.

The men stood around in small groups and exchanged news and views, as well as swap stories. However, some couldn't outtalk their wives and had to sit in the courtyard with them until the concert was over. The band usually quit playing around nine o'clock and then the ladies caught up on their visiting too.

We teenagers could hardly wait from one Saturday night to the next. We thought the days would never pass. We girls walked the north and west sides of the square at least a dozen times, for this was where most of the activity was. We hoped the boys would notice us and perhaps ask to take us home. Oftentimes they did just that.

When cars came in, people would go up town or come into town, if they lived in the country, and park their cars at the curb on these two sides. Then when they grew tired they sat in the car and watched people pass by.

Some townspeople were known to go up before supper, park the car and then walk back home. Thus, they were assured a place to sit.

Both the West Side Bakery and Hurt and Bonney's on the North side had ice cream parlors. The round tables and chairs used there are now collector's items and sell at fabulous prices. I wonder what became of the child's set at the Northside Bakery.

No Saturday night was ever complete without a visit to one of these parlors for a sundae, a cherry phosphate or a limeade. We really felt we were in the money if we had the extra cash to have nuts sprinkled on top of the sundae.

After the visit to the bakery, the boy friend walked us home, if we lived in town. Later, when cars began to appear we sometimes were taken home in his dad's car. What a thrill that was!

And then began another seemingly endless week until the next Saturday night rolled around.

Lamar's Ladies World War I Band 1916-1918
Arthur Walters, Directed and Trumpet Player
Ida Gibson Walters, Clarinet
Ocie Elam, Clarinet (Snook)
Eula York, Clarinet (Harmon)
Eula McCrea, Alto (Schreiner)
Mavan Cuseberry, Alto (Schubert)
Virginia Brigham, Trombone (Elam)
Emma Mammen, Tuba
Babe Bridges, Drums
Gertie Oldham, Trumpet (Stockdale)
Mrs. John Wagaman, Sr., Clarinet (Hazel Hughes)
Roth Faubin, Trumpet (Unable to be in the Service)

Lamar's First Uniformed Band
G.A. Seyffert, Leader
Charles Parry
E.C. Grant, Mr. Eggars
George Pool, O. Hast

Lamar's Band In 1915
Arthur Hays, Harry Hays
Jud Porter, Arthur Walters
Reggie Wilson, Drums
Ocie Elam, Clarinet
Virginia Brigham, Trombone

From Democrat May 20, 1909
Lamar's Band Members
Arthur Walters, Leader
Tracey Fast & Leroy Guinney, Coronets
John Schopf, Earl Daugherty & two
  Scraggins Boys Played Alto

Oscar Cox and Fred Hays, Drums
Archie Smith, Clarinet
Dick Weed and Carl Lonenecker, Trombones
Victor Walters, Baritone
Chick Weed, Tuba

It Happened Here

September 13, 1984

As we sat on the square evenings during our recent Fall Festival and watched the crowds walk by, I couldn't help but think how fortunate we are to have this big annual event in our town.

We can thank our founder, George Ward, for insisting we have a large square and an equally large courtyard park, as he called it. Otherwise, such a celebration could not be possible there.

Then, my thoughts wandered back to some of the other interesting, exciting and even tragic events I have seen happen down town in past years.

Naturally, I thought first of the fun I had all those Saturday nights during the band concerts. Next, I recalled the many July 4 celebrations when crowds, and I do mean crowds, poured onto the square each year to enjoy the Independence Day festivities.

And yes, I remember that fateful July 4, 1928, when the truckload of fireworks parked at the northwest corner of the courtyard exploded sending people scurrying in every direction.

At least 50 injured, some severely, and others not so severely. Many were trampled in the rush to get away and one lady, Mrs. James Webb, lost a foot. What a horrible experience that was!

Then there was the joy and excitement when we heard the Armistice had been signed ending World War I, Jerry Cronin filled his two seater Ford with young people, friends of his two daughters, Alice and Ruth.

And would you believe that he, as well as others, drove their cars with horns honking and everyone yelling down the west side? No, we weren't upon the graveled street. We were right upon the sidewalk next to the buildings.

It turned out that we had celebrated prematurely, though. The Armistice really was signed two days later, November 11, 1918. The celebration was then repeated but the city fathers decreed, "no more driving on the sidewalks."

Who could ever forget the excitement when the "boys" finally came home and paraded around the square for all to see? What a day that was! Even with all our happiness, our hearts sorrowed for those who did not returned and there were several.

Another thrill packed time was when everyone who could possibly get to Lamar came to see some exciting history take place. We even drove down from Kansas City where we lived and many others came great distances as well to witness the formal notification and response of Harry S. Truman that he had been chosen by Franklin D. Roosevelt as his vice presidential running mate.

At the time, 1944, editor Aull said it was the largest crowd ever to gather on our square. Though, I suspect that Saturday night of our recent Fall Festival might have surpassed that number.

What a thrill it was to see this happening right before our eyes. We were all pleased that Mr. Truman had chosen his birthplace for this important event.

I recall there were many prominent political figures here, but the one I remember best was Texas Senator John Connally. He attracted attention because he looked like he had forgotten to go to the barber shop.

Today, we wouldn't likely notice the hair down on his collar, as his always was.

It is a fairly safe bet that no future generation will be privileged to witness a similar historical event here and especially in front of our courthouse on the west side.

Last, but not least, was that fateful May 28, 1919, when Jay Lynch, who had shot down in cold blood our sheriff, John Harlow, and his son Dick, was hanged by an angry mob in a tree just north of the courthouse. The tree has since died and been removed.

How, I, as 18 years old, could have stood right there and watched the whole proceedings, I'll never know. I wasn't the only one, though, for the crowd was huge!

No doubt, some of you other old timers can call to mind other important events which took place on our square. These are the ones that impressed me most.

If only our downtown buildings could talk.

Our Street Names

October 25, 1984

One day Phil Hurst suggested I do an article on our street names. He had been looking at the first, as well as later plats of our town in the recorder's office and noticed the many changes over the years, which I dare say few of us know about.

I have read several times that our streets had no official names until 1884 and that it was after the building of the two railroads throughour county that the city fathers deemed it important to bestow legal names on them.

They may not have been official, but the streets have had names since the original plat was made in the George Ward home in March, 1856, and since the first addition (Peters) was platted shortly thereafter.

What we now know as 9th, 10th, 11th and 12th (160), were given the name of Congress, Mill, South and Greenfield Road, respectively, on that original 1856 plat.

The Mill Street those days led to a mill. Bet you folks living on Mill now are surprised to learn your street once ran east and west. We can assume that Greenfield Road was the wagon route to Greenfield, though this is only a guess. It is rather ironic that the street is now 160 Highway and does skirt Greenfield.

Our present Cherry, Walnut, Maple and Oak are today the same as they were dubbed in 1856. As Phil says, "What can change about a tree?"

What you now know as Gulf was originally Scott, Broadway was Sheridan, Poplar was Grant and today's Mill Street was Johnson. So those on the east side of the square weren't so fortunate.

The present Parry Street was once Benton. Hagny was Lincoln and Jefferson was first Bismarck and later Miller.

When I was growing up Truman Avenue was Kentucky. This was changed, of course, to honor President Truman, who was born at 11th and Kentucky.

We also had a College Street and a College Avenue both converging on the Lamar College. Confusing? In the 1880-1882 period, Grand, Lexington and Jackson Streets were opened up and named and today carry those same names. Important events of the time, current national leaders and the passing parade of local leaders seems to have influenced the naming of our streets as well as the renaming of some of them.

In the late 1870's and early 1880's someone had the bright idea of calling the streets surrounding the square North Main, East Main, etc.

-45-

That didn't last long, though, for when the railroad came, it was decided to name the one running north from the San Francisco, (now the Frisco) Gulf Street.

So Scott, which was later West Main, was now Gulf and is still Gulf, for the same reason, the one leading to the Missouri Pacific depot became Pacific.

The council then went on to name all the remaining east and west streets by number as First, Second, Third, etc., both north and south.

Pacific was the dividing line. This resulted in much confusion, though nothing was done about it until the early 1930's.

Then the council abolished the name Pacific and starting at the extreme north boundary with First Street, went on south to the city limits by number. Pacific now became 10th.

By the way, do you know where Arthur Aull Road, Brother Adams Drive, Allen Avenue and Howard Drive are? It is a nice way to honor past and present community leaders, isn't it?

So folks, don't let anyone tell you our streets weren't named until 1884, for it just isn't so.

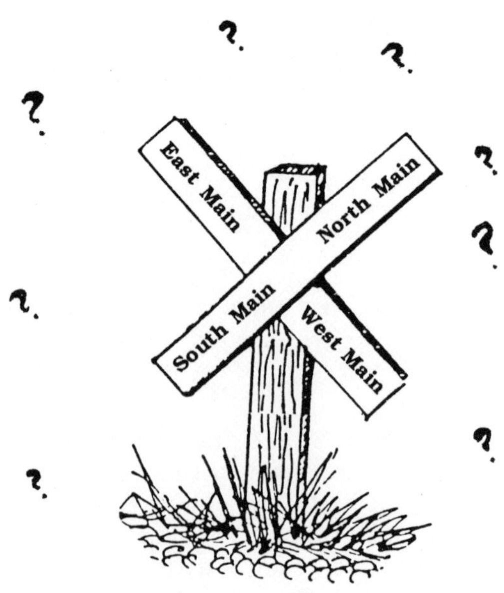

Colorful History Of Traveler's Hotel Told

February 1985

One of the main topics of conversation these days is the razing of the old hotel, which most people living here now know only as the Travelers.

There are many misconceptions about its past history, including when it was built, who built it, its name at various times as well as who the different proprietors have been.

After months of research, which means dozens and dozens of telephone calls, interviews with oldtimers and hours of reading legal documents, I can now give you the true story.

So, no longer does anyone need to wonder or guess. My special thanks goes to J.D. Pahlow, who so willingly gave of his time to help me and to Jennetta Burch, Happy Turner and Stew and Lucille Fry as well as the many others who shared information with me.

The hotel was built in the later part of 1897 and the early part of 1898 by R.J. Tucker and W.R. Banks, two very active and prominent businessmen in the early days of our town. On August 20, 1897, they borrowed $8,000 from Farm and Home Association of Missouri for the purpose of erecting the building.

Daisy Griffin Love remembers when the construction was being done. As the family walked to the Baptist Church each

Sunday morning they always observed the progress of the past week.

Eugene Stark, who was nine years old at the time, says he and his older brother, Norvall, kept the carpenters busy running them away. It was so much fun to step from joist to joist; he said.

For some reason, Tucker on July 20, 1898, deeded his interest to Banks, who on that same day sold to the Lamar Hotel Corporation. Mr. F.D.W. Arnold (Frank) was president of this company and Annie Bridges, sister of the Arnolds' adopted daughter, Babe Bridges, was the secretary. In the transaction, mention was made of buildings and improvements, so we know the hotel was already built.

The Pickwick Hotel was now ready for business and opened with Arnold and his wife, Sarah, as the first proprietors.

Mr. and Mrs. Gerrit Snip and family arrived here from Illinois in December, 1900. They could not get immediate possession of the farm which they had purchased through the popular land agent, C.Y. Trice, so the family stayed at the Pickwick for some time.

Loretta Snip Wolf, though just a little girl, says she remembers the parlor, which was the southeast corner room on the second floor. The music box on a table in the center of the room made quite an impression on her. She also recalls that she thought it quite exciting to go down the stairs to the dining room for all their meals.

Arnold hired Earl "Happy" Turner in 1912 to work as a cleaning man. He, along with Jesse Tucker and Charles McClain, worked there for several years. Happy has many memories of these years.

He says the hotel was known then as the $2. establishment. This meant the room was 50 cents a day and each of the three meals was 50 cents. You couldn't stop in and get just a cup of coffee those days. (The regulars at the Do-Nut shop wouldn't like that, would they?)

Many a little girl went there for music lessons from Babe, who was a talented musician. She was also quite a horsewomen. Many of us remember the large painting of her on her horse, which hung at the top of the stairs, where anyone in the lobby could see it. We wonder, too, what became of it.

The Arnolds remained at the hotel until the Lamar Hotel Corporation sold it to J.C. and Cora Jackson on May 22, 1916. The Jackson renamed the hotel, calling it the Jackson.

However, on October 3, 1918, they sold to Mary and L.S. Ryan. In a legal paper dated September, 1922, it was called the Travelers Hotel, so it was this family who gave it the name we know it by today.

Emory (Stew) Fry went to school with Tommy Ryan, a son, so he remembers the hotel as it was then.

H.C. and Pearl Chancellor, parents of Richard Chancellor and Margueritte Tucker, purchased the hotel from the Ryans on April 25, 1930 and operated it until July 1951, when son Harold took it over.

Jenetta Burch started working as a maid in 1941 while the Chancellors were there and remained for 37 years, so she saw many proprietors, as well as tenants, come and go.

It was during the latter part of the Chancellors' ownership that the coffee shop was installed. The space that had provided the Chancellors an apartment and a beauty shop on the extreme north end, operated at various times by Lola Gardner, Daisy Cox and Lucille Fry, became the new coffee shop. some of the early day managers were Joe Shelton, Crip Coiner and Sue Vaughn.

Earlier Lucille Fry had been a waitress in the dining room. Those were the days, she said, when the tablecloths and napkins were white, meals were served in three courses and the table was cleared between courses.

Before coffee shop days, the cooking was done in a kitchen behind the dining room. I recall that Ella Fitzhugh began cooking for the first Arnolds and continued there for years. She was the mother of Lavonne, a classmate of mine, and of Guy Keyes, whom we all remembered as just about the most handsome young man that ever grew up in Lamar.

Harold and Elsie Chancellor sold to the Henson Corporation on September 12, 1952, and they are the ones who sold to the Foster sisters, Versah, Letha and their mother, Myrtle, on June 8, 1953.

They did a lot of remodeling and restoration and operated a fine hotel. No door had ever been cut between the coffee shop, kitchen and the dining room until they had it done. (The old kitchen had long since been abandoned.) I remember that the waitresses had to carry the food through the lobby to the dining room. Imagine that!

The Fosters operated it until January 6, 1969, when they sold to Edward and Maxine Gilmore. It was the Gilmores who sold to Ralph and Pearl Arnold on October 11, 1974. I believe they are the ones who gave it the name Travelers Inn.

Arnold had hopes of restoring the building to its former grandeur but ill health plagued him. He passed away in the second floor room that had once been the pretty parlor Loretta Wolf remembered so well.

On July 7, 1978, John and Bernice Buchanan and Clyde and

Hazel Weston became owners. However on January 8, 1979, the Buchanans sold their half to Mark Weston. Everyone agrees the Westons really updated the hotel serving delicious meals and giving excellent service in every way.

On May 20, 1981, the Westons sold to William and Lucille Powell and on March 24, 1983, Max and Jeanie Britt of California bought the business.

Foreclosure proceedings were started January 30, 1984. Sales were held later to dispose of furnishings and also parts of the interior such as the two beautiful stairways.

The hotel was a fine establishment in its earlier days, serving the public in many ways. In fact, at one time there were three doors across the front, not counting the southeast corner ones.

The middle one opened into a room where drummers, now called salesmen, could display their wares to prospective buyers. in later years, a wall was removed and this space became the south part of the coffee shop, after having served for a time as the Chancellors' apartment.

For several years, the banquet for the Fall Festival Queen contestants was held there. The judges sat in the dining room and observed each girl as she came down the stairs, precious memories now for these girls.

In fact, all through the years, this was a favorite place for large banquets, for club meetings of all kinds, as well as family and high school class reunions. I recall the BPW and the Kiwanis met there for years.

If the old walls could have talked, they would have related many happenings there and would most certainly have told us of important people who were once guests there. Among them would have been the early country singers, Hank Snow, Porter Wagoner, and also Bill Monroe and the Blue Grass Boys from Nashville, Tennessee. Harry Truman engaged a room when he was here for his formal notification that FDR had chosen him for his running mate. While he used the room to freshen up, he did not spend the night there, according to Jennetta Burch.

Yes, the old hotel has a proud history and it served the public well for many years (not 100 as some think.) One service everyone appreciated was that it was the bus stop for a long time. This was such a convenience both day and night. No standing outside those days waiting for someone to come for you.

And so, with a sad heart and tears in our eyes, we bid adieu to a landmark we shall all miss and shall never forget.

The Pickwick Hotel

F.D.W. ARNOLD, Proprietor

CHRISTMAS MENU.

Cream of Chicken Soup

Oyster Stew   (Fresh Oysters On Ice)   Plain Celery

Queen Olives   Pickles

California   Grapes   Bananas   Apples   Oranges

———

Roast Turkey Dressing   Plum Preserves

Baked Domestic Goose   Apple Sauce

Boiled Sugar-Cured ham, Horseradish

Roast Sirloin of Bee, au Jus

Baked Duck   Cranberry Jelly

———

Fruit Salad   Stuffed Dates

Jelly Tarts   Watermelon Preserve

———

Mashed Potatoes   Creamed Cauliflower

Browned Sweet Potatoes

French Peas   Stewed Tomatoes   Cold Slaw

———

Plain White and Graham Bread   Creamery Butter

———

Vanilla Ice Cream

Devils Food Cake   White Cake   Fruit Cake

English Plum Pudding   Wine Sauce

Pumpkin Pie   Lemon Pie

Blackberry Pie   Home Made Mince Pie

Cream Cheese

———

Tea   Coca   Milk   Coffee

CHRISTMAS DINNER 50 CENTS

Menu From
The Pickwick Hotel

A History Of The Lamar College

July 25, 1985

We did, indeed, once have a co-educational college here and for many years it was the major contributor to the educational community and a focal point for cultural activities.

In 1889, Mr. Dave Beamer, manager of the Missouri Immigration Association, actually a real estate company, here in Barton County conceived and formulated a plan for giving this section of the state a splendid college where young people could have educational advantages without having to go so far from home. Being a shrewd businessman, he knew this would be a talking point and trying to induce people from other states to buy land and move to our county.

I might add that Mr. Beamer also was instrumental in getting the present Saint Mary's Church built to replace the small frame one originally built in 1869, which had stood first on Grand Avenue in Parry's first addition.

Both these ideas worked and many families, including Catholics did move here, especially from Iowa and Illinois. Some descendants still live in the county and have been the backbone of our community all these years.

And so, he built the large two story brick and stone building with a basement and tower, atop a hill overlooking the southeast part of Lamar. It actually was on a part of his farm. To this day that farm is called College Hill farm by many and the area where the school stood is still called College Hill.

It was an imposing structure and as a writer back in 1905 said, it had been the pride and joy of the entire community for 17 years.

It stood at the east end of what you now know as 17th Street, through it was College Street back then. There was also a College Avenue running north and south. Both these streets converged at the college.

The landscaped grounds were shaded by handsome trees, all of which made the scene on College Hill stand out as a most beautiful area.

According to records, the institution was first placed in the hands of Professor James K. Hull, who managed it successfully for several years. Later, a Judge Main took the reins.

Students came from most of the surrounding towns, as well as many from Lamar. Transportation was by horse and buggy unless the pupil lived close enough to walk back and forth.

Old timers recall that the girls played basketball on one side of the lawn while the young men used the opposite side for football. They had some outstanding football players too, one being a fellow named Langenecker (wasn't it Carl or was it Ed?)

The team was so good they even played Kansas University, as well as the teams in surrounding towns.

After a time, the institution failed to come up to Mr. Beamer's expectations, so he decided to take over its management himself in 1896.

On August 26, 1897, a large ad along with a good picture of the college appeared in the Southwest Republican newspaper, published by F.D.W. Arnold. It stated that the Lamar Education Association would open the college again on September 15, with full college courses taught by able educators. It also said there would be a strong normal or teacher's course and that emphasis would be placed on the commercial and musical department.

For a time the college did well. A picture in one of the centennial issues of the Democrat showed the class of 1903 with 30 members, all young men except two. However, as far as I can find out the class of 1904 had only seven girls graduating and no boys. That is hard to understand, isn't it?

Do you recognize the names of any of these 1904 graduates, Eva Heath (Box), Rose Tucker, Bess Beamer, Myrtle White, Lucy Ford (Spencer), Jean Delores Fulkerson and her sister Florence?

The college at this time had six instructors.

The summer school held for teachers fared much better, as many took advantage of the courses designed to better prepare them for their work.

As the years passed the attendance dwindled and finally in 1906 the building and contents were sold to the Benediction Sisters of Atchison, Kansas. A parochial school and a so-called academy or college was opened on September 2, 1907, with the Benediction Sisters in charge. After a time it was called St. Joseph's College.

Sister M. Digna Krenner, O.S.B. at Atchison wrote to Dorothy Gastel in 1980 that the school was actually a grade and high school and that the term college did not necessarily mean the four years of study following completion of high school.

It was really a boarding and day school for girls and young ladies. Boys were admitted until they finished the eighth grade, but only as day pupils, according to the recently published history of Saint Mary's Parish. By the way, one of these boys who attended was Phil Roth and he is still a parishioner of the local church.

Students not boarding in private homes or living at home stayed with the Sisters at the convent which was two blocks west and one north of the college.

There were no facilities for food at the school, so many took their lunches with them each day. However, those living close enough went home for their mid-day meal. Matie Rudisale (Veale) said she walked everyday to the home of Mr. and Mrs. Creecy at what is now 14th and Broadway, where she boarded. "That lunch hour really went fast," she said. Sister Elizabeth was directress of the school and was assisted by six other nuns, as well as other teachers on the faculty. One of these was a Miss Anna Drake who later became Mrs. Bayard Rhodes. Old timers all remember what a talented lady she was.

Children's classes were held in the two north rooms of the first floor while the older pupils had their classes in the rest of the building. The music conservatory and the art department occupied a house about a block north of the college. It burned many years ago. Sister Martin told me recently that she went to the conservatory for music lessons though she was not a student at the college.

Quite a number of local young women attended the upper classes, many of whom were not Catholics. No effort was ever made to interfere with their religious beliefs, though the Catholic religion was the one recognized by the institution.

Do you remember any of these graduates in the classes of 1907 and 1908, Marie Markwick (Konantz), Reba Carlton (Foster), Florence Tuck, Oshia Elam (Snook), Irma Rex (Woodward), Olive Staats, Eula York, Florence Stark, Vesta Van Scoyk (Hooten), Evaline Scott, Dora Elam, Grace George, May Cox, Fern Brown, Marie Dicks or Matie Rudisale (Veale)?

After about five years of ownership the school was closed as there wasn't enough attendance to make it worth while any longer. I read an article not long ago that said the handsome structure was torn down shortly afterward, which is an error. All throughmy high school years as well as several years before and after, the popular pastime of young people on Sunday afternoons was to walk out lovely tree lined College Street (17th) to the old school which then stood vacant. We took Kodak pictures, talked, and just plain had a good time congregated there on the wide front steps.

My youngest sister, Mabel Babbitt, remembers going to dances there, so evidently the auditorium was rented occasionally through those years while it stood vacant.

Finally around 1927, according to Marvin VanGilder, 15 years after its closing Josh Box razed the building and tower leaving only the foundation and the front steps. Many of these bricks were used on the construction of Memorial Hall. Which was built in honor of Barton County World War I veterans who were either killed in action or died in military service.

The George Dighero family has lived for a number of years in the house which now stands where the college once was. The only reminder left of this beautiful building are the front steps and even they aren't as long as they once were.

I am sure there is much more that could have been said, but it has already faded away, a victim of Father Time.

I could not have written this much history without the help of a former teacher of mine, Matie Rudisale Veale, one of those who graduated in the class of 1908. She still has a good conduct medal given her by the Sisters, as well as commencement programs, pictures and other mementoes which she so graciously shared with me.

Early County Fairs.

August 8, 1985

While searching through old newspapers recently for information on our former college, I ran across two accounts of fairs held here many years ago.

Since our annual Free Fair is fast approaching, I thought you might be interested in comparing how they were handled back then with ours today.

One was an article titled "A Four Day Fair" which was in the August 26, 1897, issue of the Southwest Republican Published by F.D.W. Arnold. This fair was held in Early October and not when it was hot as blazes.

It seems the people had said they wanted an old fashioned county fair with livestock, agricultural, garden and domestic products to be given honored places on the premium list. (We still do this.) And yes, there was to be hurdle racing, chariot racing, trotting, pacing and running races. Bicycle races were to be held, also.

Premiums would be offered for the best buggy team, best lady rider, etc. I wish they had listed what was to be included in that "etc."

The chariot races were to be contests among the different townships and the hurdle races were to follow the old fashioned plan (whatever that was) and were to be open to all.

The article did go on to say that in hurdle races, rider and horse had to clear barriers, fences, ditches and other obstructions. That would have been exciting to watch!

J.A. Potter of Barton City Township and Sam Hackney of Newport were to be the managers. They stated they had the Fair well organized and insisted the four days would be a star spangled all round success.

The other article appeared in the Daily Democrat on July 5, 1902, and was titled, "The Fourth and Street Fair."

It describes an entirely different kind of celebration. It was a street fair and not one held at the fairgrounds as the other was.

Remember, the square had not yet been graveled, so there had to be a lot of dust to contend with throughout the celebration. I imagine the water wagon was kept busy sprinkling the dusty streets. The article started out by saying Friday was the star day. Early in the morning, wagonloads of people began pouring into town from every direction.

The writer believed there were at least 8,000 people on the square by 2:00 p.m., not withstanding the fact it was the first week in a month that farmers could get into their fields.

The merry-go-round, always popular with the children, took in at least $300. On the southwest corner of the square, Mount Pelee's eruption could be seen. The editor thought it the best exhibition for the money and felt it didn't do as well as it should have.

Oh yes, there were "Hooche-Kooche" girls who did a fair business. I suspect they would have done better if the wives hadn't kept such a close tab on their husbands.

Barlow's Minstrels were popular as was Mr. Midget, who acted as a valet for a little brown dog that was trained to do many stunts.

Of course, there was a palmist who was kept busy reading the palms of many a girl and her boyfriend. Colonel Kemp and his Indians gave a good, free show, just as he said he would.

About a thousand people took advantage of Colonel C.Y. Trice's famous free telescopic view, which was erected on a post in front of Adams' Furniture store (about the middle of the west side) George Harshberger, who was in charge, urged everyone to avail themselves of the free show.

When one gazed through the telescope, he said, far up on the steeple of the courthouse, (yes, it once had a steeple) a white canvas, which bore the following advertisement. "A complete abstract of all the land in Barton County as shown by the records in this edifice."

How about that for a unique and catchy advertisement?

At least the thousand who looked through the tin tube learned that Mr. C.Y. Trice was in the abstract business. I'm surprised J.D. Pahlow hasn't thought of doing this.

The article closed by complementing Mayor Wells, his special police force, the management and Colonel Kemp for their efficient work. It didn't mention the managers' names, however.

These two fairs certainly don't sound much like our Free Fair of today, nor were they similar. Some say they would like to see a few old time events added.

Perhaps our antique display and the two races held on Saturday will fit into that category. How about catching a greased pig next year?

Our Changing Landscape

February 27, 1986

I often wonder if the younger generation realizes how the face of Barton County has changed since the early 1900's. Nothing ever stands still and this is quite evident in the many changes that have taken place in our landscape since my girlhood days.

I really miss the two story houses and the large barns we used to see in the country. A barn was a necessity when farmers had to depend upon horses to work their fields and when they had their own milk cows. Not so today!

Surely, no old timer has forgotten playing in the barn loft where the hay for winter feeding was stored and wasn't it fun?

By the way, how long has it been since you saw a huge haystack on a farm? We children enjoyed burrowing holes into which we would crawl and hide from each other. I often wonder what my grandfather Lee who died in 1914 would think of the big round bales we have nowadays.

Most every home in the county had a vegetable garden back then. No farm wife would have been caught buying fresh vegetables for her table in the summertime. How many gardens in the towns or in the country do you see today?

Besides the house and barn on the farms, there were usually several other out buildings, each serving a definite purpose.

Yes, there was a chickenhouse and pen (I can still remember my mother going out for a chicken for dinner and having it dressed and in the skillet in a short while.,) a small house where the meat was cured, a butchering shed, a wash house for doing the laundry, a small barn for the milking, a tool shed, a place to keep the firewood dry and yes, the hog pen with attached shelters.

And who could ever forget the privy, or the outhouse, as some called it. Very few had bathrooms then.

Then there was always a wood pile near the kitchen door and close by a little pile of kindling for starting the fires in the stoves.

Most every home had a cistern, as well as a rain barrel to catch rainwater from the eaves.

This soft water was great for doing the laundry. We also had wells somewhere in the yard and barn lot which provided the drinking water for both the family and the stock.

When windmills came along, that changed, and how welcome they were.

How many of the above mentioned do you see today? As the need for these vanished, so did they. Sometimes, we do see an occasional outbuilding, but you can be sure it has a different use now.

I am always saddened when I see an old house or barn slowly falling down. What interesting stories they could tell us!

At one time, every township had what we called a country school. Now they are gone, as are many of the rural churches.

Rural electrification and rural water revolutionized the life of farm families. The pretty homes with attached garages, security lights, well kept lawns and machine sheds are what we see today, as we tour the countryside.

Wouldn't Rip Van Winkle be petrified it he were to awaken now and see the cars whizzing by on our blacktop highway?

I recall the time when all roads in Barton county were dirt, and that included the new highways 71 and 160. People were really happy when they were graveled and then when concrete came into use, they thought they were in hog heaven, forsure.

Louis Niehaus was the first man in our county to use gravel. He hauled it from the creek on his farm and spread it on nearby roads. You can be sure that was a popular direction to go when the boyfriends took you for a drive on Sunday afternoon.

At one time every village and town had at least one blacksmith shop. For awhile, we lived in Milford, where Prine Thomas was one of the village smiths.

We girls looked forward to stopping a few minutes on our way home from school to watch him pound those red hot horseshoes into shape.

We always waited expectantly for him to ask us his usual question, "Are you going to have tater soup for supper?"

As I drive over Lamar, I can't help but think of the many changes in our landscape here. So many of the two story houses are gone, and in many instances, were replaced by the then popular bungalow and its outside garage.

Then we had a good many vacant lots but today they are as scarce as hen's teeth. Would you believe that the ground where the hospital now stands was once Mr. Taylor's orchard?

Many homes in town had a small barn for a milk cow and for a horse or two if they had a buggy or surrey.

We had a coal shed for, by that time, we were heating and cooking with coal. Often times there was another small building which was usually called a smokehouse, but which was really for storage.

I still miss the steeple that was once atop the courthouse. The chain link fence around the courtyard has long since been removed, for with the advent of cars, no one drove horses into town.

These and the loss of the big elms in the courtyard and over town changed the landscape a lot.

The wells and the pumps on the square were discarded long ago. And yes, the big scale that was once at the southwest corner is no longer there, either.

The two railroad depots, the tall standpipe out on North Truman, the Opera block, the Park (later Colonial) and the Traveler's hotels, the livery stables, the calaboose and east Pacific (now 10th), the old mills, the broom factory, Evilsizer's cabinet shop, Seyffert Carriage Works, the Bijou, the old college, the Exchange Hotel (later Lamar House) where Wyatt Earp was first married and the many white buildings at the Fairgrounds are just some of the familiar places now gone, all of which changed our landscape immensely.

Most of the original church buildings have been replaced by nice brick ones. The three grade schools and old Central High have long been gone. The only early day school left is the one for Negro children at 14th and Grand.

We don't see many silos or windmills these days. Nor do we see that big bell mounted on a post near the kitchen door to call the menfolk to dinner. Even all the old iron bridges are gone, except one, I believe.

All these changes make me wonder what Barton County will be like 85 years from now. It will look different, that's for sure. Be nice to be around just to see, wouldn't it?

An Old Fashioned Front Porch

(Remembering)
The Big Front Porch

June 5, 1986

When I was growing up, most every house had a big front porch. Sometimes it extended around one or both sides of the house a bit. As I look around today, I realize these are fast disappearing.

Back then, we thought a house didn't look finished if there was no roomy porch. Some said this was as necessary to a house as a slice of onion is to a hamburger. Suppose that is why some of the new homes being built today do have a good sized porch?

Most porches I remember had either a clematis, trumpet, or honeysuckle vine climbing up on the wood or chicken wire trellis. These provided a little shade, and also perfumed the evening air somewhat.

I don't recall much fancy furniture. There were usually one or two old rockers and perhaps a few splint seat hickory chairs. When company came, or the family gathered, more chairs were brought from the kitchen.

During my teenage years, most everyone had a porch swing suspended from the ceiling with heavy chains which always squeaked--well almost always! I daresay many a romance began on these swings, helped along by the soft moonlight **and a twangy** ukulele.

There was no possible chance of sitting out there with the boy friend past eleven o'clock, for those darned chains announced our presence. We knew we would get called in and, what an embarrassment that would have been!

The big porches served many purposes in their heyday. It was a perfect place to sit a spell and cool off after hoeing in the garden.

And what a better spot to hull the peas or string the green beans for next day's dinner? Yes, green beans did have strings that had to be removed back then. It was a tiresome chore, and even though we did our best, we usually missed a few strings.

The men of the house often sat on the front porch to read the day's newspaper while supper was being prepared.

The children got washed up and were told to sit on the porch and to stay out of the mud (or dirt) until time to eat. I recall a certain aunt who threatened to scrub four little girls' knees with a corn cob if they didn't stop getting them so dirty.

Sometimes neighbors sauntered over in the evening to discuss the state of the crops or the possibility of rain. Many a decision about the best candidate for the Presidency on down to the local sheriff was settled right there on the big front porch.

Since there were no televisions, radios, or air conditioners, everyone congregated on their porches in the evening to keep as cool as possible. It was an ideal time to discuss the events of the day and perhaps visit back and forth with the neighbors on both sides. How much of this is done today?

Our house was the gathering place for our friends on sultry-summer afternoons. Since there were four of us sisters, we sometimes had quite a group. What fun we did have those days!

There was no such thing as Pepsi, Coke, or Sprite, so far as we knew, and so it was lemonade for us. We seldom had ice then either, but the well water was fairly, cool and we didn't mind.

If mother was low on sugar, we could always depend on our neighbor friend, Tinner Bart (actually Alfred "Tinner" Klein) to run home and bring back enough from his grandmother's sugar bucket. My how good that lemonade tasted on those hot afternoons! Sometimes I wish I could relive some of those fun-filled times!

I suppose television and air conditioning have been factors in causing the demise of the gracious front porch. Even those remaining, and those being built today, are seldom used as they once were.

Once in awhile, though I do see someone sitting on his porch, and I am reminded of Gladys Riddle who always seemed to enjoy hers. Then I've noted that the "girls" at Granny's Boarding Home make good use of that one, which also has a porch swing.

Spring Housecleaning

July 31, 1986

Having recently finished the spring cleaning of our little red house, my mind hearkens back to many years ago and how differently it was done then.

Housewives usually began this annual chore just as soon as it was warm enough to take down the heating stove. This was always the cue, too, for the children to ask if they could not go barefooted. Women then, as today, prided themselves on having a clean house and would do their best to finish before their friends.

The parlor was the first room to be cleaned and the heating stove had to be out of the way first, what a chore that was!

Invariably some soot that had accumulated in the stove pipe would scatter over the room. Have you ever tried to clean up soot? If so, you know how difficult it is. The stove was cleaned inside and out, polished and then relegated to a bedroom corner where it was covered over for the summer.

I remember what a job it was to do the polishing, for there were no rubber gloves then to protect hands and fingernails.

Tacks were next removed from the rag carpet along the walls. The strips were separated, washed, dried and then sewed together again. As I look back, I wonder how in the world they washed those long strips, for their only equipment was a wash board and a tub. Before the carpet was tacked down again, fresh straw was spread on the floor. If that wasn't available, newspapers were used.

Some years later, Axminister and Brussels rugs became popular and every house wife had at least one of these beautiful creations, if at all possible. They got dirty, too, and were either hung across the clothesline or spread on the ground and given a good going over with a carpet beater to remove the loose dirt.

In the meantime, the white lace curtains were washed with homemade lye soap (later Crystal White or Pandy) and were starched so stiff they could almost stand alone.

Since there was no ready made starch, the housewife made her own with flour and water which she cooked awhile and then strained to remove the inevitable lumps.

It was a chore to iron them so they would hang straight. So the lady of the house really welcomed curtain stretchers when they appeared in the stores. Oh yes, many women obtained their curtains by saving the signatures from the sacks of Arbuckle coffee.

The beds and bedding were always cleaned thoroughly. When a family moved into a house, they often had to fight bed bugs, for they were a common problem those days.

The usual method was to dip a large feather, one from a rooster's wing was ideal, into coal oil and run it along the top of the baseboards being sure to get plenty behind it. The bed rails and the ends of the slats were also given a good dousing.

Eventually, there were no more bed bugs, though it took several applications of the coal oil. By the way, coal oil is called kerosene today.

Each spring the straw ticks were emptied, washed, and then refilled with new straw. If straw wasn't available, they used corn shucks, so says my aunt Emma Boles. The new straw was sort of prickly until pressed down with use. We felt rich when we had accumulated enough feathers to have a feather bed atop each straw tick.

Part of the house cleaning ritual was to carry both the feather beds and the feather pillows outside to air.

Sometimes, it was necessary to wash both the ticking and the feathers in the pillows. What a tedious job to transfer the feathers to a cloth sack, sew up the end, and then wash them in the tub..

Harder still was to get the wet feathers dry. After much shaking up and several days of hanging outside, they were ready to go back into the clean ticking. The family now had fresh pillows again.

Seventy-five years ago, most people in Lamar heated and cooked with coal. Smoke would pour out, if there was any blaze at all, when more coal was added. The daily task of emptying the ash pan was a dusty one. No wonder housewives had difficulty keeping the house clean.

The walls really collected the soil from the stoves. Back then, most people used wall paper instead of painting as we do today, I remember that paper hangers were quite numerous but try to find one now.

Our mother always tied a clean white rag over her broom and wiped the walls down. Later, we had a commercial cleaner - a soft sponge like substance which cleaned the paper quite well.

The kitchen got its share of going over, too. A search was first made for mice holes and when one was found a tin can lid was nailed over it immediately.

I remember once that mother failed to clean the kitchen chairs well enough before she freshened them with varnish. As a result our dresses stuck to them for weeks. Wonder what that would do to the man made fibers of today? The floor was usually the last to receive a scrubbing.

Since water had to be carried in from the well and sometimes wasn't too plentiful, any suds remaining from the wooden floor scrubbing was used to scrub the privy. Lime was scattered inside the seats and the past season's Sears and Roebuck or Montgomery Ward catalog was placed in a handy spot.

By this time, the housewife breathed a sigh of relief for her house cleaning was completed for another year.

Aren't you glad you weren't keeping house back then?

Rub-A-Dub-Dub!

October 27, 1986

Today, I filled the automatic washer with a load of soiled clothing, turned it on, and in just a few minutes everything was washed and ready to be put into the dryer. Almost before the breakfast dishes were done, the bell was ringing and telling me it was time to remove and put the garments on hangers. Not one required any ironing. All of this took place in a short time, as you well know.

This set me to thinking about how the laundry was done down here in the Ozark foothills when I was growing up. Back in those days, washing and drying the clothing and linens was practically an all day task, especially if there was a large family.

We always had to strain the wiggle trails out of the water in the rain barrel before heating it on the kitchen stove. This was soft water, which made it much easier to get the clothes clean. During prolonged dry spells, we had to use water from the well in the back yard. This was always hard and had to be softened with soda, climalene or something similar. Some people had cisterns and that did away with this problem.

If you have never scrubbed dirty clothes on a wash board, using home made lye soap, you are fortunate indeed. I can tell you for sure, it was a back breaking job and hard on the knuckles and wrists, as well.

White clothes were always boiled in the old iron boiler to keep them white, or so we thought. During the summer, we set the boiler on two rocks out in the back yard and built a fire underneath. We girls had to take turns punching the clothes down to keep them under the water.

I remember so well what a task it was to empty the sudsy water out in the yard, and then carry up fresh from the well for at least two rinsings.

Mother tied a few balls of blueing in a small square of white cloth. This little bag was then swished through the second rinse water several times until the desired blue was achieved. Woe unto the one who got it too blue!

Nearly everything was starched in those days and since commercial starch was unheard of, we had to use a flour and water mixture, thinned with boiling water and then cooked awhile. Yes, there were always lumps, that had to be strained out.

What a chore it was to get the laundry dried in the winter! Few had basements to hand things in, nor did we have furnace heat. If it was too cold to hand them outside, they were strung on makeshift lines or draped over chair backs when the warmth from the parlor heater and the cookstove would eventually dry them. What a mess that was!

It was a different story in the summer, though, as we would hang outside on a rope or wire line (always saggy), stretched between two trees. The towels and rags were spread on the grass or over bushes so the sun could bleach them.

Ironing was a big chore too, for everything had to be ironed those days. For years, the housewife ironed on the heavily padded kitchen table. She thought she was in seventh heaven when she got a legless ironing board which she could place between the table and a chair back, or else between two chair backs. Some folding wooden ironing boards were made as early as 1905, but not many here had them until years later.

What do you suppose our grandmothers would think of the drip day we have today?

I suspect you young mothers would collapse if you had to use the heavy flat irons housewives used then. Later, a lighter weight one with a detachable handle was popular.

Even worse, was the hot fire that had to be kept going in the cookstove to heat the irons. Imagine, if you can, what it was like doing the ironing on a hot summer day with no electric fans and not even air conditioning!

Electric irons came in about 1920 and what a blessing they were! Though, somewhat crude electric washers were on the market as far back as 1907. They were not common here until the late 1920's or early 1930's.

Grandmother would likely faint dead away if she could know that her wash day equipment is now being purchased by collectors. Early day tin wash tubs bring higher prices than do the old galvanized ones and the older wooden wash boards are preferred over either the glass or brass ones which came along later. The benches that held the tubs are bought up today, refinished and used as coffee tables in family rooms. I've seen some used thus and they are charming!

My goodness, I should have put another load of clothes in the automatic washer long before now!

Lamar's Opera House

February 5, 1987

Yes, Lamar once had an Opera House. It wasn't a separate building as most were, but was a part of what was called the Opera Block, and was on the south side of our square.

It was a large three story buff brick building and was erected by C.H. Brown and William Avery in 1881 and 1882, at about the same time the two railroads were being constructed through the town. It truly was an impressive building for that day and people were proud of it.

The street floor consisted of businesses. Among the earliest proprietors were Ryan and Kennedy, the Golden Clothing Company, McCutcheon and Jones and a W.V. Lemon. There was a wide stairway in the center of the building which led to the second floor.

The front part upstairs had several offices, including that of the building manager. There were also some shops. Around 1900, two Green sisters taught china and oil painting up there. I remember well when a Mrs. Joe Lethgo had her dressmaking shop just to the west of the stairs. My mother, as well as several other women, sewed for her and made the big sum of $5.00 per week. Sometimes ladies took their material to the shop and she would help them make their garments. Then I also recall that a Mrs. Mitchell, who later married the prominent Charles Glenn, had a millinery shop upstairs, also.

During World War I, the office space to the east of the stairs was converted into two apartments. Mr. Thad Wills and his daughter Lorene (Sis Martin to us) occupied the one to the east and the one nearest the stairway was rented by Dr. Bailey, an Osteopath, who had both his office and living quarters there.

The Opera House, itself, occupied the back part of both the second and third floors. The front part of the top floor served as headquarters for Company C National Guard.

The main floor of the Opera House, where the audience sat, was 40x60 feet. The stage was at the east end and back of it were five dressing rooms. I recall that the huge mirror in each had bright lights on three sides. There was no gallery or balcony, as many Opera Houses had those days.

So far as I know, very little of the stage property still exists. Mrs. and Mrs. Dalton Harris have two of the chairs from a parlor set and the late Marble Douglas had the matching love seat, which I believe is now in the possession of her daughter, Ruth Webber. The audience chairs were a Windsor type with a rather high back. Don and Peggy Klein do have two of those and Edith Klein has a third one.

The baby grand piano was owned by the late Mrs. Wallace Griffin for a number of years. Eventually, Jess Turner got possession of it and the last we knew it was in their yard where the twins, the dogs, cats, birds and the weather had free rein.

In its heyday, the building had a series of managers. Some of these were Dave Beamer, C. Bert Avery, W.R. Banks, and Guy Earp and Ray Wilson who served jointly as did Mr. Beamer and Mr. Banks during World War I.

At one time the Opera House was the center of all cultural and recreational activity for Lamar and the surrounding countryside. We were treated with musical comedies carrying their own bands and orchestras and Negro minstrels with either all white or all black personnel. They were never mixed.

Then there were the melodramas which always drew capacity crowds. E.J. Mann tells of one that required a live horse on the stage. Watching the men get that horse up and down the stairs was an exciting experience for a five year old boy.

Of course, "Ten Nights in a Bar Room" was produced as well as "Uncle Tom's Cabin." Daisy Love told me of one time when the latter was here and how much she wanted to see it. Since her father, D.K. Griffin, had been a Confederate soldier, he would never allow his children to see the play. Usually, there was a small parade around the square on the afternoon of the show to create interest.

One time Daisy managed to slip up town during the parade and she described it thus: A miniature log cabin was set onto a wagon bed and two mangy mules were pulling it; they were followed by two blood hounds straining at the leashes being held back by a stern looking man holding a big whip in his hand. Daisy ended the story by saying she never knew how little Liza got away.

Occasionally, a Shakesperian troupe came to town, and then there were magicians, hypnotists, concert singers and famous pianists.

I remember so well the young man who had been hypnotized and rode a stationary bicycle for several days in Galloway's Clothing Store window, first door east of the stairs. When it came time to awaken him, he was taken upstairs to the Opera House stage where a large crowd saw him brought out of the hypnotic state.

Another memorable experience was getting to see and hear the famous Negro Blind Boone. My, how he could make that piano talk! By the way, he really was blind.

We had home talent shows regularly. Sometimes professionals were hired to train the local people.

Betty Aull White said her father, Arthur Aull, played either Caesar or Marcus Aurelius in one of these. She wasn't sure which character he played. Another time, her mother had a cat in a basket as part of her act. The cat jumped out and about broke up the play.

Bess Thurman, daughter of Judge B.G. Thurman, was an active participant in these home talent shows. Her wedding to Tom Braniff, founder of Braniff Airlines, at the Thurman home on South Gulf was one of the big society events of the town.

Many lectures and political speeches were heard there, also. In fact, there were community gatherings of all kinds, including society dances.

It was the custom to have at least one community children's play each year. In 1912 "Mid-Summer Eve" was presented and just about every child in town had a part. The next year, "Four-Leaved Clover" was featured. I note from the program that the admission was 25 cents.

For years, the high school classes presented their plays there. The senior class plays were always big events. Teenagers would form a line before the ticket office and wait all night in order to get choice seats. My class of 1919 presented "And Home Came Ted" for its senior play.

Graduation ceremonies were also held there for years and until the high school had facilities to handle these events.

The day came when Mr. E.E. Wagner opened his picture show called, "The Bijou." Such theatrical groups as the Dubinsky Brothers began coming in, erecting a big tent where Memorial Hall now is and presenting a different play each night for a week. As

Lamar's Opera Block

a result of all these attractions, the Opera House wasn't used as much as in the past.

Basketball games were played up there for some time and then there was also a skating rink for awhile. Finally, the Gray Manufacturing Company took it over and made tents, awning, etc.

In its last days, the building was owned jointly by Smith Long and Joe Springer. The Opera block now had the tent factory upstairs and on the street level there were the paramount Studios managed by Ray Miller, Bill Davis' Oklahoma Tire and Supply, Mr. and Mrs. Joe Shelton's Cafe and the South Side Billiard Hall, operated by Don Darrah.

Carl Schmitt's Appliance Company joined the Opera Block on the east. The following businesses finished out the block to

Broadway. Fowler's Cafe, Palace Drug Store, a picture show, Dr. Karl Kraty's Office, The Lamar Leader (a newspaper) and lastly, the Lamar Steam Laundry.

The Egger Bank building erected in 1881 by Fredolin Egger, father of Thomas Egger, was the only building to the west of the Opera Block. The space on the Gulf street where the Post Office now is, was a vacant lot then.

Early in the evening of windy May 4, 1943, a customer in the Billiard Parlor saw smoke in the back of the Opera Block and turned in the alarm. The fire was believed to have started near a coal shed at the back of Gray Manufacturing Company. Before it was over, the Blaker Lumber Yard, The Baptist Church and the entire Opera Block were gone and one-half million dollars in damage resulted.

The Egger Bank (now Pahlows) building suffered some damage, but due to a fire wall, it did not burn. Because of the terrific heat and the high wind, most every business building on the square had someone stationed on the roof all night watching for flying sparks.

The Carthage Fire Department came to help and Wayne Pierce, son of a former Lamar Baptist minister, was killed and two other Carthage fireman were injured.

Ruby Weidman told me about a man going to the roof of the Opera building to watch the fire, never dreaming that building would be destroyed, too. She couldn't recall his name, but I learned later it was Bob Seeman. According to Ruby, the fire was consuming that building so fast by that time that he almost didn't get rescued.

And so, ended the existence of a building that had been a center of culture for years, and which touched the lives of everyone in the community in many different ways!

Lamar and Barton County
"Firsts"
May 7, 1987

Several who were absent when I gave this as a program recently for the Rotary Club, asked if I would write it for the newspaper. So, here it is with a few additions.

If you have been thinking the present Courthouse is the only one we have had, you are wrong, for it is the fourth one.

The first was a wooden structure two stories high and located a little to the east of the middle of the north side of the square. Records say it was built about 1858. It was later used as a restaurant.

By 1860, the community had prospered to the extent it could afford a permanent structure in the center of the courthouse lawn. It was a two story brick building with four rooms below and court rooms above. It had a center hall running north and south on the first floor. In part of the east side, Mr. George Ward, town founder, published the very first newspaper in Barton County. James Cook was the first editor, followed by John Mallory.

In November 1862, this building was destroyed by fire. Some of the records had been removed and buried under a smokehouse at the farm home of a Mr. Wells, who lived south and a little west of the village of Milford. They were damaged considerably, but some could be copied and are now in the Recorder's office.

Some of the bricks from the foundation were used in constructing the Fred Fuhr home west of Lamar. After it was demolished, a daughter, Helen Fuhr Wilson gave the Historical Society a few of these bricks. They can be seen in the museum.

In 1866, after the Civil War was over, a temporary frame building was erected in about the center of the west side for around $6,000. This served until the present one was built and was then sold and moved.

The fourth and present one was built in 1889 for $32,500. As you know, it is an imposing edifice of native Barton County Stone and St. Louis red brick. The iron work was done by the Lamar Iron Works and included two beautiful spiral stairs. Does anyone know where this iron foundry was located?

A misguided county court removed the steeple back in the early 1920's. They also removed and sold one of the winding stairs, thereby preventing the county from ever getting it placed on the National Registry of Historic buildings.

The first organized church services that we know anything about were held in the northside courthouse. The Baptists were the first to erect a building for worship, and I have read that this was done about 1870.

The first school in the county, according to old records, was two miles south of Lamar and was made of logs with only one-half of it floored. The children sat on split log benches.

The first teacher was a William Seals and a descendant of his, George Seals, lives at Opolis, Kansas. He attends Historical Society meetings when he can.

According to records, the first school building in Lamar was a one room frame building built in 1866 and located at what was then one block east of the southeast corner of the square. I have reasons to believe that building is now Edith Klein's Kitchen.

The first store in Lamar was a small building located where the Lohmeyer-Konantz Funeral Home is today. It was operated by George Ward, founder of the town.

The first brick building on the square is the one where Denim and Lace is now. It always housed drug stores until recent years.

The first saloon was erected by a Billy Brown in 1857 and it was located near the middle of the north side.

Our first Post Office was in the home of Joseph Parry, son-in law of George Ward. The little white house still stands at the northeast corner of 11th and Mill, although it underwent some remodeling a few years ago. All mail those days came from Independence to Papinsville (wherever that was). Riders on horseback went to Papinsville for the mail.

The village of Lamar was incorporated in 1867 and for a number of years, it was under the supervision of the County court and was managed by a board of trustees, one of whom was chosen chairman to serve one year only.

On February 11, 1870, two thirds of the inhabitants petitioned the court asking, they have a separate government from that of the county. This was allowed, though the village still used trustees to manage its affairs.

One of their very first acts was to hire Wyatt Earp as the first constable at a monthly salary of $15. Then in march, 1870, an ordinance was passed forbidding hogs to run loose. It was repealed in May, as it couldn't be enforce.

In 1881, the very first elected mayor, Charles Van Pelt, took office for a two year term only. Until 1905, no mayor could serve longer than two years. Since I researched just to 1905, I don't know how long that rule was in effect.

The Lamar Water and Light company was formed in 1887, and

the tall standpipe out on Truman Avenue was built to hold the water from Muddy Creek. Sixty hydrants were placed about town for fire protection. The standpipe was removed in 1954.

The first electric light also appeared here about 1887. However, it was years before all households had electricity and running water. Some of the lights were arc, the rest were electric.

In 1866, German born Gustavus Seyffert came to Barton County and founded a carriage and wagon works on the corner now occupied by Gilkey Ford Company. He was a cousin of the great German composer, Wagner, and was quite musical himself. He established the first dance band here and also was conductor of the local band which played for various occasions. All old timers remember his daughter, Mrs. Charles Edwards (Clara.)

The town began graveling the streets in 1882 and it took many years to get the job done. Mr. Louis Niehaus was the first citizen to spread gravel from the creek bed on the roads by his farm.

The first railroad through here was the one that runs through the south part of town. It was constructed in 1879-1880. Just a year later, the Missouri Pacific came through running north and south.

Our square was not paved until about 1928 and would you believe the city fathers wanted to pave just the center, leaving the sides gravel? Mr. Authur Aull, Editor, put up quite a fight in the newspaper and won. So, the square was paved curb to curb.

The REA came to Barton County about 1937 and farmers rushed to take their kerosene lamps and lanterns to the cellar, attic or dump. Mr. Elza Smith tells a story of what happened on the Floyd Morey farm. The lights were turned on in his milking barn before herding the cows inside. However the shadows and the bright lights frightened them and not one cow would go inside. He had to turn off his new lights and get out the old lanterns in order to milk the cows that night.

At one time, we had two telephone systems here - The Guinney company came in 1902, and in 1910, Southwestern Bell also moved in. Imagine the confusion? I recall some business places having two telephones.

E.E. Wagner opened his picture show on the north side of the square -- a few doors west of the center. I recall going there a few times. He then moved in 1909 to the Tucker Banks Building at the southwest corner of the square, and still later, about 1922 or 1923, he had moved to 104 N. Broadway.

The first woman to vote in Barton County was Lucretia Van Pelt. I have heard her tell of trudging up town in the cold to vote at 6 a.m. on the November 1920 election. She is now a resident of Lakeview Nursing Home.

The first undertaking establishment so far as I can find out was operated by Mr. Hoyt Humphrey in the rear of his hardware store, located at the southeast corner of the square. Some of his early death and burial records are still available.

The first, and so far as I know, the only legal hanging, was in 1891. An Amos Avery had killed a traveling salesman and was found, tried and sentenced to be hanged. We have had two other hangings that I know about, but they were not legal ones.

The very first Dazey Churn was made here in Lamar in 1885 by a Mr. S.J. Sullivan.

The first person to die in our new hospital which was dedicated October 2, 1947, was Mrs.. Clara Connor or was it 1949?

Next, is a more recent first! Gerald Gilkey is the very first car dealer to have a franchise for both General Motors and Ford in the same location and using the same personnel. How about that?

In closing, the largest crowd ever to assemble in Lamar was in 1944 when Harry S. Truman was officially notified that he had been chosen by Franklin Delano Roosevelt to be his vice president. History was made here that evening.

The Commercial Hotel In It's Hayday

Commercial Hotel's Colorful History Told

June 1987 (Heritage Edition)

There has been much speculation about the Commercial Hotel at 9th and Gulf since it was purchased by the Lamar Democrat. People are wondering when it was built and whether it is as old or older than the Traveler's Hotel recently razed.

So, because of this interest, the request of several people and the fact we want this information for our Historical Society records, I spent many hours delving into its past history. My thanks go to J.D. Pahlow, Armilda Stockdale, Leita Boas, Jack and Zelda Metsinger, Margaret Jones Lucas and several others who were willing to share their information.

On April 16, 1857, President James Buchanan signed the Swamp Land Act, enabling Arkansas and surrounding states, including Missouri to receive from the U.S. Government certain swamp and overflow lands, which were supposedly unfit for cultivation.

And so, on May 16, 1858, Jason Bruffey, land commissioner of Barton County, sold a tract of this land to Joseph C. Parry for 75 cents per acre. The lot where the hotel now stands was a part of this area and is legally described as Lot 4 and Block 4, original town of Lamar, Missouri.

For many years, lot 4 and the adjoining lot on the south were bought and sold together.

On September 24, 1866, Octorus and Sophronia Pyle purchased both lots for $250 and in December of that same year, they sold to David J. Lindley and William R. Vanhoosen for $3,000. This indicates a building had been erected somewhere. The following year, William Lindley purchased the property for $4,800.

It wasn't until 1882 that official records contained any mention of a structure on either lot. At that time, O. Ferguson and wife sold Lot 5 to S. R. Crouse and after the legal description, the agreement said, "the same being known as the Eagle Hotel property." So, we presume, but cannot prove that this is the building erected back in 1866 by the Pyles.

Evidently, this hotel was later named the Gulf, for it, too, was on Lot 5.

For years, a small house stood between the two hotels and was occupied by an elderly lady whom everyone called Granny Smith.

In 1897, The Lamar Daily Leader carried an ad stating the Gulf Hotel served meals for 20 cents or $3.00 by the week, with good meals and accommodations. Some of us old-timers have a slight recollection of both the little house and the wooden hotel on Lot 5.

On November 24, 1882, S.R. and Josephine Crouse sold the corner lot (4) to Orlando Ferguson and his wife for $241, and on May 22, 1885, they sold it to George W. and Mary J. Johnson for $6,800, which tells us again that a building had been erected.

On January 10, 1891, Ella G. Smoot purchased the property for $10,000. The transaction stated that it was known as the Commercial Hotel property. This was the first time in the official records that the name Commercial Hotel was used.

After this, there were ever so many owners. Some sold quickly at a profit, while others held it for a few years before selling. And yes, some even lost the property by foreclosure. Some owners operated the business themselves, while others leased to various people.

Pearl Pahlow (now Humphrey) and her sister, Carrie, spent their first night in Lamar at this hotel.

In 1906, the John Pahlow family moved from their farm to the new home on North Gulf Street, now occupied by J. Digby Gifts. Bed time came before enough beds could be set up, so the two girls were elected to spend the night at the hotel. John and Susie Duden were the proprietors then.

The 1911 Barton County Directory has an ad which says "Commercial Hotel-H.J. Poff, proprietor, Best $1.00 a day house in the city. Nice rooms and plenty to eat. North Gulf Street, one block off the square on main road to the Fairgrounds." Then at the bottom of the ad were these words, "Gulf House second door south annexed to the Commercial Hotel." Could that explain the doorway at the southwest corner which is now blocked up?

Margaret Jones Lucas, granddaughter of the Poffs, told me her parents, Leora Puff and William "Bill" Jones, were married in the hotel parlor in 1911. She also said her grandparents served family style meals for 25 cents.

In 1920, S. L. Pattison and wife, Lou, sold to J.M. Bayne, who then sold to Clyde and Ethel Morton.

Leita Smith Boas, who worked for the Mortons, said they did not serve meals, so the patrons ate at one or the other of several nearby cafes.

During the ownership, the dining room just back of the front office was furnished with a long, double-width table on which were placed pens, ink, pencils, etc. The salesmen who stayed there when in town, used this room for their bookwork.

The second floor was used by the traveling men and the overnighters with the exception of John Slavens, a permanent guest. He had a habit of smoking in bed.

One night, it caught on fire and the whole hotel had to be evacuated for a while. Can't you just see the men and women in their long white nightclothes crawling out the windows and sliding down the ropes? Even though the ropes had knots tied fairly close together, I'm sure it was a scary experience.

The third floor accommodated the other regulars who paid by the month. Leita recalled that Ross Wattenbarger and Ray White were two of these.

She also said the parlor, opposite the office, was a beautiful room, but seldom used. The door was kept closed to keep the patrons out. The double doors on the front were kept locked so everyone had to enter by way of the office.

There was a big potbellied heating stove in the office and Leita says she remembers so clearly how Mr. Slavens always tapped his pipe against the edge of the coal bucket.

On June 20, 1932, the Mortons leased the hotel to J.D. and Minnie Cummins. They agreed to pay $60. per month, take good care of the premises and keep it free from filth, from danger of fire or any nuisance. Because they had children to help with the work, Leita was no longer needed.

On November 25, 1938, Mr. and Mrs. Charles Hagins purchased the hotel from Fred and Gertie Gray. Their daughter, Ollie Hagins Metsinger operated it during their ownership.

Jack Metsinger says he was his mother's bellboy and furnace tender. He remembers he had to go down several steps to the furnace room at the back of the building. Above this was a storage room. Signs of his addition are still quite obvious, though the upper part has long been removed.

Jack also told me that during trials, the jury stayed there sometimes a week or more at a time. They slept in the two front rooms on the second floor with extra beds brought in to accommoderate them. The jurors even ate their meals to themselves, as they weren't allowed to talk with anyone else. In case you are wondering, this was the day before women jurors.

Each bedroom on the second floor had a lavatory, while the tenants up on the three had to use a big white china bowl and pitcher. Which held the water for their daily sponge. For a time, only the second floor had a full bathroom, according to Jack.

Mrs. Armilda Elrod Stockdale has written an interesting article about the years she worked for Mrs. Metsinger. I understand it is to appear in the paper. I don't believe she mentioned that her one and only tip was 15 cents given her by Mr. Ed Moore, a lawyer here.

Helen Dockery (now Foley) who lived out Milford way worked at the hotel for her room and board while in high school. Since she now lives in California, I was unable to interview her. No doubt she could relate some interesting stories.

Several different times through the years, Mr. and Mrs. Curley Hosselton operated the hotel for its owners.

Their daughter, Zelda, now Mrs. Jack Metsinger, said her folks served their meals in individual dishes, instead of family style. The meals were 35 cents and a monthly ticket was available if so desired. This was punched for each meal eaten.

Don Viers's mother, Bessie, was a long time cook there and according to Zelda, helped rear her.

Zelda also recalled that Negro Jim Webb, the local cab driver and highly respected by all, always ate his meals in the kitchen. She, also ate many of her meals with him, she said.

W.R. Lewis and wife purchased the hotel November 3, 1943, and sold it to Ira W. Boss, April 11, 1945. Mr. Boss did not serve meals, though he rented the rooms, mainly to older men.

Some of the women here told me that when they were in high school, they didn't like to walk by, even on the opposite side of the street, because there was usually a row of men sitting along the hotel front whose pastime was to stare at the girls.

Carl and Ethel Martin became the next owners on July 17, 1956. They discontinued the hotel part and instead operated "The Martin Tobacco Store" selling liquor, also, I believe.

John and Ethel Jakobsen operated it a short time after Mr. Martin died, later selling to Paul and Helen Lewis.

And you know the rest of the story! Yes, it is now owned by the Lamar Democrat and is safe at last from the demolition crews!

Since the Travelers was built in 1897-98, this hotel is over 10 years older---so settles that question!

The Old Commercial Hotel Purchased By The Democrat in The Spring Of 1986.

Life In Milford In The Early 1900's

July 30, 1987

When I was growing up, Barton County was dotted with lively little villages, One of these was Milford, 12 miles northeast of Lamar, lying so peacefully at the foot of a hill with Horse Creek meandering along only a short distance to the east.

I have always felt that C.M. Wilcox, who liked the country so well when traveling through that he decided to stay, was a wise man, indeed. On November 15, 1869, he filed the plat for a Village.

It was he who gave it the name of Milford as Milford Connecticut, was his home town.

He wasn't the first settler in the vicinity, though, for John Henry Cook had brought his family from Tennessee in 1857 and settled three miles south of where Milford was to be. About the same time, Jacob Cummins Faubion acquired land which is now the east part of the village.

Levi and Mary Boles were operating a little store near the

Milford School taken about 1909. Ruby and I are in this. She is 9th child from the right and I'm 12th. I have a white belt. George Cass was the Teacher.

branch about 1/4 mile south of the future Milford, according to their grandson, the late Reed Boles.

Jack Purinton says the James Reynolds family had also arrived and had settled on the farm he now owns, 2 miles south of the village.

The Rectors and the Broadhursts were also there, according to old records. I'm sure there were others that I don't know about.

My maternal grandparents, Jim and Dora Lee, lived in Milford when I was very young and I had the good fortune to spend a lot of time with them. After my parent's farm home burned, we lived for a time in the east part, later moving about 1/2 mile south to the Spencer place, better known as the Benny Farrell farm - though it was an earlier house. As a result of these early years there, I have a wealth of memories - some pleasant and others not so pleasant.

I recall three very active churches - Presbyterian, Southern Methodist and Disciples of Christ-Christian. On our way home from Sunday School one morning, we passed another church and heard a woman shouting loudly as she testified. It frightened us children so, we ran all the way home. We learned later, it was a woman, who lived east across Horse Creek, and who quite often got "carried away" at the service.

There were four general stores then. The owners were J.M. Herlocker, Frank Faubion, a Mr. Vandiver and Ed Boles who was next door west of the drug store which my grandfather Lee and Dr. Tom Duckett owned jointly. Reed Boles worked for his uncle Ed. When he saw my sister, Ruby and me passing the store, he would call us in, give us each a piece of candy and ask us to take a note to our Aunt Emma Lee. Of course, he made us promise not to read it and we never did - not even once!

I remember two blacksmith shops. One was operated by John Werts and his sons, Clint and Clarence. The other smithy was Perrine Thomas. It was the latter who invariable asked us girls as we passed, if we were going to have "tater loup for lupper." I learned later there was a young man in town who couldn't sound the letter S. Every time he saw my Uncle Sam Lee, he would say, "Lam Lee, are you gonna have tater loup for lupper?" Needless to say, that soon became a common expression around Milford.

We think a Mr. Ryan established the old steam powered grist mill on the north outskirts. It was still standing, but in a dilapidated condition when I was little. I remember the tall weeds almost hid it from view.

A. Mr. E.W. Jenkins lived in a little house located where Mrs. Fay Lee's home now stands. He made splint bottom chairs and

The Milford Band in 1910

rockers for about every woman in the area. Some are still around, I might add.

Just to the south of the old mill, Mrs. Clara Capps and her children lived. She was the telephone operator when you wished to talk with someone, you rang one long ring and then told her whom you wanted. My favorite friend those days was Dolly Capps, her daughter. We sat together at the school, for then, we only had double desks. Mrs. Jack Purinton is the daughter of Vernie Capps who married Joe Gibbs. Another daughter Bess married John Gibbs.

I remember a little about Mr. and Mrs. Perry Taylor who were the great-grandparents of May Gardner and Edith Klein. In the Barton county 1911 directory, Mr. Taylor is listed as an undertaker. However, he was also a shoe cobbler and finished coffins. His shop was in the back part of the building, where my grandfather had a hardware store after selling his drug store interest to Dr. Duckett. This building is used as a home today.

Mr. William Mitchell and sons came to Milford and established an undertaking business in 1914.

And would you believe Milford also had a hotel? In 1907 Sam and Rinda Chapman were the operators. Across the street there was a newer mill as well as a livery stable. The Ed Schneiders later operated all three of these businesses. All signs of the mill and stable are gone, but the old hotel remains. I believe it is occupied now as a home.

And yes, the village had its own photographer - Crosby Thomas, whose shop was in a room of his home. Crosby was a brother of Perrine, the blacksmith. By the way, the latter's son Elmer, better known as Pete, lives here now.

In 1903 Milford had an outstanding baseball team whose manager was Ed Faubion, father of our local Marvin Faubion. And in 1910, they even had a top notch band whose leader was Ira Alexander.

Application was made for a Post Office in 1886. I have no remembrance of where it was located in the early 1900's. I do recall that my Uncle Rob Lee was the very first mail carrier out of Milford. He drove a team and mail wagon, similar in looks to the rigs the Amish drive today.

I shall never forget the night lightning struck the Herlocker Store which was located where Esther Chapman's Store is now. People grabbed buckets and rushed to help fight the fire. I remember, too, that all cisterns and wells were pumped almost dry, but to no avail.

Another frightening experience was when Hattie Ligon's little boy fell in the well and drowned at the home of his grandparents, Mr. and Mrs. John Gibbs,Sr. Those piercing screams were heard across the field at my grandparents' home will remain forever in my memory.

I was spending the night with my cousin, Hazel Faubion, when Halley's Comet passed over. We were so frightened because we thought everyone would die in the night. Imagine our surprise

Milford First Mail Carrier Rob Lee

when we woke up next morning and realized that we were still alive!

One dear lady in town had mental problems. At times, she was herself and then she would be off completely. One night, she tied bed sheets together, slid to the ground from the second floor and disappeared for several days. We children were terrified for we expected her to jump out and grab us any minute.

We were having Thanksgiving dinner with my uncle and aunt, Rob and Lola Lee, one day and our dessert was to be blackberry pie. Oh how good it looked! But -- we tasted coal oil in our very first bit. Aunt Lola had filled the tank on her coal oil cooking stove and evidently didn't wash her hands well enough before making the crust. I can just see her grabbing up our pieces and throwing them out. So, that was one Thanksgiving without a dessert!

We four sisters had Diptheria when we lived on the Spencer place. Dr. Tom Duckett came out to see us one morning and his son, Claude fresh out of medical school was with him. Dr. Claude always said we were his first patients.

The oyster soup suppers in the Lodge Hall above the drug store and the ice cream supper held in the summers on the then vacant space between Frank Faubion and Ed Boles's Stores were social occasions for adults and children alike.

Many of the men were prominent in the affairs of our county. For instance, Simeon Isehnower was a member of the County Court when our present Court House was built in 1888. His name is on the cornerstone. This I don't remember.

As I think back to those early days, several ladies' come to my mind immediately. I know it was because they were so good to us children. Those were - my own grandmother, Dora Lee; my great-grandmother, Sarah Winkle Howell; my great-aunt, Dora Hudson Faubion; Susie Croley Walker, whose son Fred now lives in the Central Chapel area and lastly Jose Gibbs, my mother's close friend, and mother of our local townsman, Pat Gibbs.

People born in the vicinity of Milford and Newport have been called Horse Creekers ever since I can remember. I can't claim to be one, though I'm often called that by Marvin Faubion, Floyd Gardner and others.

What is undoubtedly the largest barn constructed on a farm in this part of the state was built by Mr. James A Jaycox in Milford Township in the late 1880's.

This barn was built for use as a still, but never used for that purpose. This may explain why the lumber used was shipped from Minnesota and Wisconsin as floors, walls and a four-foot wide stairway were so carefully finished. Yellow pine was used for floors and white pine for box stalls. Sliding doors were formed of solid wood.

So large is this barn that a fully loaded wagon can be pulled into the barn, make a circle and leave without ever backing up. Stalls were provided for at least 20 horses and stanchions for 15 to 20 cows. Baled hay was stored in the north and east loft with loose hay on the south. Grain was stored on the second floor with chutes to carry grain to the box stalls for daily feeding.

Jacob A. and Mary E. Rector purchased the farm where the barn stands, in 1909, from the Jaycox estate. Edith Klein, a granddaughter of the Rectors, furnished information about the barn for this article.

A sense of history seems to prevail over Milford and the surrounding area. A few years ago, David Cruickshanks from London England visited us. We took him to Milford so he could see where many of my relatives had settled years ago. He was quite taken with Chapman's Store and the way the men gathered around the stove in the back end to discuss the latest news, solve world problems and tell their latest jokes.

Before David left for England, I asked him if there was any place he would like to see again and he said "Yes, I want to go back out to Milford." So, even a Britisher sensed what I have always felt.

Even though it is no longer the Milford of my childhood, I hope it never disappears, as so many other such villages have.

The Old Galvanized Washtubs Were Household Necessities During The Early 1900's

November 12, 1987

No description of life in Barton County during the early 1900's could possibly be complete without some mention of the important place galvanized tubs had in our lives. Fact is, they were a household necessity and every family I knew had at least two. These tubs were made of steel which had been coated with zinc. The housewife really welcomed this new kind, for they were much easier to handle than the heavy wooden ones used previously. Tin tubs were on the market for awhile, but they dented too easily, so soon lost favor.

While tubs served several purposes in the home, one of the main ones was for doing the weekly laundry. One held the hot suds for scrubbing the soiled clothing and linens on the wash board and the other was used for rinsing out the suds. I would just as soon forget how many times we had to carry the water from those two tubs out into the yard and then re-fill with fresh water, before the laundry was ready to hand out on the clothes-line.

Tubs were also used to catch rain water from the down spouts on the house. The women liked this soft water for washing their long hair. What we called bobbed hair didn't come in style until the early 1920's. This rain water was great, too, for dish washing as well as for other cleaning chores.

I'm sure you old timers remembered the popular party game called "bobbin' for apples." The tub held the water and the apples for this lively game.

Since very few homes had bathrooms those days, the galvanized tub was brought into the kitchen or some other room, placed close to the stove and partially filled with hot water for our Saturday night baths. Papers were always spread around the tub to catch the inevitable spills and splatters.

It wasn't such a chore in the summer, as dish pans, large kettles and buckets of water were placed out in the hot sun all day to warm the water. During cooler weather, it had to be heated on the stove.

We children dreaded those winter baths, for it was torture to undress by the hot stove, blistering on that side and freezing on the other. Before we dared get into the water, we tested it by very cautiously sticking in as little as we could of one foot, we always feared we would scald it and sometimes, we almost did!

I doubt if you of the younger generations have any idea how hard it was to squat into that tub and try to get ourselves clean enough to pass our mother's inspection. Finally, we were in and when some part of the back touched that cold steel, we squealed like a fresh stuck hog! We knew it would happen, but it still was a shock.

Imagine, if you can, what it was like to step out of that warm water and stand by the hot stove, dripping and shaking, baking on one side and chilling on the other, while we worked frantically to get ourselves dry.

Since it was such a chore to fill the tub, every child in the family usually took his bath in that same water, with the occasional addition of hot water. How clean do you suppose the last ones were?

The time came when we flatly refused to squat into that tub another time! From then on, it was "spit" baths for us. I can hear you saying, "What is a spit bath?" Well, today you call such sponge baths.

This reminds me of the fellow who once said, "If I had my druthers, I'd druther eat a bug, then to take my Saturday night bath agin' in a galvanized washing tub."

When not in use, these tubs hung on the back porch (all houses had back porches then.) Woe unto anyone who put something else on those nails!

So, these are some of the ways the tubs were used in the early 1900's. I often wonder what became of all of them. I do know one way they are used today, but I'll let you figure out what that is!

Trials, Tribulations Of Childhood

February 11, 1988

I believe most of us adults are prone to think of childhood as a carefree and totally happy time. However, as I look back on my own, I know we children had to endure many annoyances and trying experiences other than the wash tub baths, I've already written about. Of course, there were happy times, too, so growing up was not all problems.

All of us little girls had long hair which we wore in braids hanging down our backs and tied with pretty hair ribbons. Can you imagine how it hurt when mother combed it each morning before rebraiding it? Getting the tangles combed out after the weekly shampooing was sheer agony, especially for us tender headed ones.

Then there was that horrible long underwear which every one wore in the winter. We would get so frustrated trying to get the legs folded over so they would fit into the tops of our shoes without too large a bulge. Seldom did we succeed. Next, we had to pull up those ugly black ribbed stockings and fasten the tops to the supporters on the underwear. What a chore all this was!

We didn't like the black sateen bloomers we put on next, but we soon found they were handy to hide the underwear legs which we tucked up under the elastic as soon as possible after getting away from home.

I understand there was once a group of girls living in the south part of town who made a practice of meeting at the court house rest room to take care of this matter.

Can you imagine the heart-break of one girl who had to continue wearing high top shoes after her friends were all wearing the new style slippers? After all, not all could throw away good shoes those days. I'm sure that little girl suffered deeply and that this was a real trial for her.

When fingered gloves appeared in the stores, many children had to continue wearing the good wool mittens, while the more affluent friends had the new gloves. How embarrassed we were! Yes, this was another tribulation.

How we children hated to wait until the adults had eaten, when we were having a family dinner! I remember thinking they would never quit visiting and finish their meal. Another worry was that they would eat everything up from us children, and sometimes they almost did.

Another tribulation those days was having to take that nasty castor oil. A little later, Epson salts came along and it was horrible tasting, too. I shudder now at the thought of either of these.

I daresay not many of you had to wear a little bag of Asafetida tied around your neck with a string or cord. Our parents thought this would help keep diseases away. It stunk terribly and I often wonder what the school room smelled like.

It evidently didn't work, for children seemed to have croup and sore throats a lot. How I hated having that goose grease and turpentine rubbed on my upper chest and throat and then that heavy wool man's sock wrapped around my neck and fastened with big safety pins. Yes, it itched, but we had to put up with it. I recall too, having to swallow a teaspoon of sugar with a few drops of turpentine mixed into it for sore throat. What a taste!

If you ever wore panties in the summer that were made of flour sacks, as most little girls did, you'll remember how embarrassed you were to have the name of the flour still showing even though mother had done her best to remove the printing. I believe our mother used Red Star flour most, for I seem to remember a big red star beside the name. Other brands used then were Kansas Best and Hudson Cream. How they would have appreciated the bleaches we have today.

Perhaps our worst trial was getting rid of head lice we had gotten at school. Few families escaped. I remember so well my mother saying it wasn't a disgrace to get lice, but it sure was to keep them.

Every day she would go over our heads with a fine tooth comb while we held our heads over a wash pan to catch any lice that fell. Then turpentine was applied followed by a good shampooing. This was repeated until the lice were gone. Can you imagine how trying this was?

How we hated those trips to the out house at night before going to bed! It wasn't so bad in the summer, but winter was another story. We'd put on our heavy wool coats, our stocking caps and when it was bad underfoot, our floppy galoshes and then we'd make a dash our there. The idea was to be there first (there were four of us sisters), so we could beat the others back to the warm room where the heating stove was.

All children went barefooted in the summer and many times we got stone bruises, which hurt like fury. Sometimes we'd accidently step on a rusty nail and then we had to have a piece of fat meat tied onto the foot to draw the poison out. Everyone believed in this then. Other times we would get a splinter in a foot or step on a bee. Then there was that mean little brother of our best playmate who delighted in throwing rocks at our feet.

Sometimes we'd be so tired and sleepy that we tried to get out of washing our dirty feet before we went to bed. Our arguing never worked though.

Going to bed in an icy room weighted down with covers must have been a tribulation, but we weren't aware of it since we knew no better.

I'm sure there were other Trials but these bothered me most.

Maybe, just maybe, I'll write an article some day pointing out the joys of being a child in the early 1900's, for there were joys, too.

Writer Recalls Family Life In The Early 1900's

March 31, 1988

Family life when I was growing up didn't bear much resemblance to the family life we know today. Very seldom did a mother work outside the home, unless circumstance forced her to be the breadwinner. So, there were very few latchkey children then.

Many days she would have an after school snack ready. Quite often, it was a thick slice of still slightly warm homemade light bread on which she had spread freshly churned butter and occasionally some jelly she had made. Unless you have eaten this, you have no idea how delicious it is.

Those days, the housewife not only baked the bread for the family, but she also spent many hours during the summer canning, preserving and pickling the produce from the garden. It didn't occur to people back then to buy everything they ate at the store.

Many townspeople and all farmers had one or more milk cows, some chickens and a hog or two. All of which supplied food for the table.

Mothers also did the family sewing, for there were no ready to wear shops those days. The children's underwear was often made of flour sacks.

I remember going with my mother into the large T.W. (Toss) Harkless store located where Fashion Crossroads is now. There were bolts and bolts of muslin, nainsook, divinity, calico, ginghams, satins, wools and taffetas from which to choose the materials she wanted. The more affluent families would have a seamstress come in and do the family sewing.

Father usually was the disciplinarian and he set the rules. When he said, "Do this," or "don't do that," the children knew he meant business. If teenagers were told to be in by 10 o'clock, they were. They knew they would be deprived of going out again for many weeks if they didn't obey.

Families ate their meals together, for in those days family members didn't have all the outside activities they do today. Children were taught to eat what was on the table, too. Not many got by with saying, "I don't like that."

One of the highlights of the year was attending the Christmas Eve program at the church. The only decorated tree the children ever saw was the big one there, for no one had a tree at home.

How beautiful it was, decorated with homemade paper chains,

long cranberry and popcorn strings and small red candles in their tin holders clipped to the smaller branches.

After the program, which was usually given by the children, Santa always came and gave each wide-eyed child a few pieces of hard Christmas candy in a small brown paper sack, some children also received a gift from their parents, which made those not so fortunate feel bad.

A social activity popular for families then was the big dinner when aunts, uncles, cousins and grandparents gathered at one of the homes to eat and visit. Long tables were often set up under the shade trees so everyone could take advantage of any breeze. These were joyous occasions, especially for the children.

Then there were ice cream socials, oyster soup and cracker feeds, square dances in the homes and box suppers at the school, as well as the Saturday evening band concerts and the County Fair once a year.

All children had chores to do, for they were taught they must carry their share of the load. There were dishes to wash and dry and always the inevitable arguing over whose turn it was.

Older children were expected to keep the water bucket filled from the backyard well. I still remember how cold that pump handle felt in the dead of winter. Then, there were the coal buckets to replenish at least twice a day, sometimes more often.

If the family used wood for heat and for cooking, there was the wood box either in the kitchen or on the back porch, which seemed always low in wood.

In some families, the children fed the chickens and also gathered the eggs. In the summer, they helped in the garden and assisted with the laundry. In fact, there were many chores children were expected to perform, even to going out to Grandpa's and helping weed the young corn plants.

One of our pleasures during winter evenings was sitting around the Round Oak heating stove eating our fill of freshly popped corn. Sometimes, we also had a big red apple. This was followed by a "study your lessons" period.

Since very few had electricity, children studied by the light from a kerosene lamp. Now, I wonder how we did it. You might try it sometime.

Older children looked forward every spring to going wild green hunting with adults. It was also fun to go blackberring in later June.

Since it wasn't fashionable to be tanned, we wore big sun bonnets, long sleeved dresses and high topped shoes to prevent snakebites.

We must have looked like scarecrows! It usually was hot and we had to contend with gnats horseflies, wasps, chiggers, thorns and those pesky snakes.

The minute we arrived home with our filled buckets, we stripped and took a soap suds bath and also put all our clothing in water to boil. We were determined no chiggers would survive. We were tired, but the visions of blackberry jam, jelly, pies and cobblers on the table later made it all worthwhile.

In the fall, some families went to the woods, usually on Sunday afternoon, to gather hickory nuts or maybe black walnuts. If it had frosted, they also looked for a persimmon tree.

As I look back on family life in my earlier years, I do believe the parents' greatest worry was that the boys would start smoking before they were 18. Many a son was offered a gold pocket watch if he would wait. It hadn't yet occurred to girls to smoke, through that worry came later.

Yes, there were many things to do those days, even if we didn't have television or radios and the sports activities. We know now. Our activities largely centered around the family.

The Lamar Ladies Band

May 26, 1988

If anyone were to ask you whether Lamar ever had a Ladies Band, the chances are you would say no. But, you would be wrong, for we did have such a band here during World War I.

So many of the band members went into the service that it was no longer possible to have the usual Saturday evening concerts in the court yard. There had been a local band here since 1889 when Gustavus Seyffert, first cousin of the great composer, Wagner, organized our very first uniformed band.

Citizens wondered how the town could possibly get along without this Saturday night attraction which they had grown so accustomed to, for that was when everyone went to town, listened

to the music, did their marketing afterward and caught up with their visiting. It was a weekly event looked forward to by all ages.

One day in the early fall of 1916, an ad appeared in the Democrat inquiring if any of the women here would be interested in forming a band to fill in while the men were away. If so, they were to contact Arthur Walters, brother of the late Paul Walters. To his surprise, several answered saying they would like to give it a try.

The youngest of these volunteers was Gertrude "Gertie" Oldham of the Forest Grove

Gertrude Stockdale

neighborhood. Her grandfather encouraged her and promised a new cornet if she learned to play well on her old instrument. She did learn and grandpa got her a new one, as he had promised.

These ladies volunteered and note that the later married name is in parenthesis, in case you knew them by their married name only. Ida Walters, the former Ida Gibson, was the first to volunteer; Eula (Harmon) York, Marian (Schubert) Cushenbury, Virginia (Elam) Bingham, Oshia (Snook) Elam, Emma Mammen, Hazel Hughes Wagaman, Babe Bridges, adopted daughter of F.W.E. and Mrs. Arnold, first owners of the old Pickwick Hotel (later Travelers) and lastly Gertie, whom I mentioned above. Sometimes, Roth Faubion, who was unable to serve his country due to a health problem, would play with them.

Mr. Walters was the director of this new group and also played the trumpet.

So far as I know, only the youngest member, Gertie (Stockdale) Oldham is still alive. Her picture appears elsewhere in this issue of the paper.

The ladies practiced all winter, according to Gertie, and by spring were able to play a number of pieces well. The difficult part was learning to march while playing, she said. But, whoever heard of a band that didn't march?

Their uniforms were attractive and consisted of navy blue pleated skirts, white middy blouses and blue silk ties. The shoes were white and the hose were blue silk. There was a fairly wide arm band on one sleeve which had the initial L.L.B. embroidered on it.

They played in the court yard bandstand every Saturday night during the summer of 1917. Gertie remembers the bandstand as a new one which had no roof, as ours does today.

After these concerts, the musicians were each given $3.00 and sometimes were taken to one of the ice cream parlors for a cone.

They met all troop trains stopping in Lamar and played for the boys while the train took on water. The teenage girls flocked to the station, too. I know, for I was one. We hoped some young soldier would give us his name and address so we could write to him. Many did and sometimes quite a correspondence developed.

The band always played in the Opera House during the big Victory Bond promotion sales. They also played in the theater at Golden City, at Oskaloosa and at other places in the county where they were selling the bonds.

Fort Scott, Kansas, wanted a band for their July 4th celebration that year, so the ladies and Mr. Walters rode the train over, had breakfast at a hotel there and gave their concert in the park later in the day.

And yes, they also played that summer at the Sheldon picnic.

That fall of 1917, they played all four days of the Barton County Fair at the old fairgrounds located where the Vo-Tech and the new high school are now. A Mr. Miller from Lockwood and a trumpet player from Carthage, whose name is now forgotten, helped the band during these fair concerts.

One day in November 1918, Mr. Walters stopped at the rural school where Gertie Oldham was teaching and told her the band was to play in Lamar at the celebration of the war's end. The Armistice was signed on the 11th, and the people in Barton County went "wild with joy." I can't remember a more exciting celebration. Some filled their cars and drove along the west side of the square right up on the sidewalk. Horns were honking, people were yelling, some were crying - all ways of releasing those pent-up emotions. The ladies band out did itself and contributed a lot to the patriotic furor of the day. From that day on November 11 was Armistice Day. However in 1954 it was renamed Veteran's Day.

The last time the band played together was on May 3, 1919, when 10,000 troops were being mustered out at Spirngfield. They went down on the early Frisco train and after arriving marched and played until 11 a.m. There were 14 bands in the parade and these were alternated with groups of soldiers - a stirring sight!

While on the packed train going home, Gertie told her team musicians that she was to be married that very next day at her parent's home to Hollis Stockdale. So, folks, this is the story of our ladies band during World War I. Everyone agreed they played a big part in helping the morale of the home folks while their young sons and husbands were "over there" helping win the war. I, for one, have not forgotten what this meant to us at home.

Historian Tells Of Past
County Court

July 25, 1988

Our county has had four courthouses. Two of these were meant to be temporary and the other two permanent ones.

Our first one was built 1857-1858, and was a temporary affair of hardwood sawed at the George Ward Mill, one mile southwest of the village. It was 60 by 30 feet, two stories high and stood a little to the east of the middle on the north side of the square. Mr. Ward, the founder of Lamar, is credited with financing this first courthouse.

Until it was ready, the court, which was organized in 1857, met at Mr. Ward's primitive home on the site of the present Lohmeyer-Konantz Funeral Home.

By 1860, the population had increased to 600. The county officials, as well as the citizens, felt they were now able to build a more efficient and permanent structure. So, a two story brick building was completed in the center of the square on the same site as our present one. It had four rooms below and court rooms above, with a center hall on the first floor, running through from north to south.

The war days from 1861 to 1865, were dangerous and tragic. The north side frame courthouse was burned the first year of the war, but the records were safe, for they had been moved to the new building, according to the 1905 Historical Edition published by the *Lamar Republican.*

In 1863, while the union soldiers, who were in possession of the town, were away for awhile, three confederate sympathizers - Bill Wells, Bill Duke and John Goss, all of whom lived near Milford, came to Lamar and removed the records from the court-house for safe keeping. Some thought they burned the buildings so the union army couldn't use it for a barracks. All we know today is that it did burn.

The same Historical Edition also said the records were buried under the smoke house of Bill Well's parents, who lived south and east of Milford. (I always thought it was Southwest.)

After the war was over, the buried records were taken back to Lamar and though somewhat damaged, were transcribed and thus saved for the county. They are now in the recorder's office. However, Record Book A and a school mortgage book were missing and never found.

Yes, there are other stories as to what happened to the records and who burned the courthouse, but this one is most often accepted as the true story.

The Barton County Historical Society has a few bricks from the foundation in their museum, courtesy of the late Helen Fuhr Wilson. The county court called for bids for another temporary courthouse as soon as possible after the war ended. Charles VanPelt offered the low bid of $5,000, and the 34x20 foot, two story high building was ready for occupancy by the end of the year. This building was on the west side of the square, where the James Burnett store had been. Know where that was??

One record says the structure was really an improvised cabin made of round logs covered with clap boards split out of green trees. It housed most of the county offices, the circuit court room and the law office of William H. Cavery and C.H. Brown, the county's first two lawyers.

By 1871, Lamar's population was well over 1,000 and the temporary courthouse was inadequate. During this year, a brick building, known as the recorder's office, was erected in the public square somewhere. No one today knows just where this was, though some of us think it was in the southwest corner of the court yard. Most of the other county offices were also in this building until around 1880, when old records tell us that some moved to the second floor of the Smith building and others upstairs in the Adams and Company Store. However, the recorder's office did not move until it went into the new courthouse, our present one.

The former west side courthouse was finally sold, moved and diverted to other uses.

An election in 1882 gave voters an option for a new permanent courthouse, but it was not until November 1887, that a proposal passed.

To the county court, composed of C.A. Morrow, Anthony Gilmartin and Simeon Isehnower, fell the responsibility of seeing that a new one was built.

They hired W.R. Parsons and Son, architects, to draw up the plans and Morrison Brothers of Lamar agreed to construct the new courthouse for $32,500. It was to be 80x120 feet and the exterior was to be of native stone and St. Louis red pressed brick. Specifications were printed in the Lamar Democrat June 7, 1888, so all Barton Countians would be informed.

The architects varied the window groupings and canopy designs on adjacent sides. The arches at all four entrances were of iron and made by the Lamar Iron Works. Original plans called for a tower with a four-sided clock and a cupola. This was built, but for some reason a clock was never installed.

The two corner stones were laid June 7, 1888. So. . .the courthouse will be 100 years old next year, 1989.

The abundant use of native stone and white trim contrasted sharply with the red brick and makes for a beautiful building. When finished it was said to be one of the largest, handsomest, best appointed and most conveniently repair, and as a result; it deteriorated until it needed much renovation.

A later court whose members were George Embery , presiding judge, Jack Davis of the eastern district and Delmar Kentner of the western were under much pressure to demolish the building and replace it with a new one.

However, after considering this from every angle and listening to the strong protests both by voice and by letter from concerned citizens who valued their historic courthouse, they decided to renovate. The work was completed in 1973.

Many of us are truly grateful to these three men, for now we have a building of which we are extremely proud and which will serve for years to come.

Barton County Lawyers and Officials 1910-1915

Front row, left to right; Thad Wills, Gene Martin's maternal grandfather; Tom Martin, Gene Martin's paternal grandfather; Paul Tucher; Ben McGilvary; Walter Evans; Harry Timmonds, E.L. Kazee, grandfather of Pat Vaughn; Ed Moore, father of Hazel Moore and grandfather of Terry and Edwin Moore; Unknown; Sam VanPool. Back row: John Slavens; Lou Casement, aunt of Eddie Casement; Bob Casement, uncle of Eddie Casement; Judge Berry Thurman, father of Mrs. Tom Braniff of Braniff Airlines; George Rumsey, clerk. (Photo courtesy of Reba Young)

In 1987, I believe, an elevator was installed at the south entrance for those who have difficulty navigating the steps. It changed the appearance, of course, but it all blends in so well with the architecture and serves such a useful purpose that people didn't seem to object. The court responsible for this is made up of Gary Frieden, presiding judge, commissioners John Stockdale and Dennis Wilson of the two districts, and they can be proud of this accomplishment.

Perhaps you have noticed that I have used the term "county court" until mentioning Gary Frieden. Just a few years ago the term "commissioner" was adopted as it seems more fitting than county court.

Visitors to our town always comment on the large court yard (it was called park in the early days,) our wide streets around the square, and our stately courthouse. Do you know that we do have one of the widest squares in the state? George Ward and the early city fathers planned well and all of us now and through he many years are and have been the beneficiaries.

And as today, we salute our stately courthouse which has seen arranged buildings in all of southwest Missouri. Barton Countians were proud of it, as they should have been. The three county court judges did a superb job.

I remember well how we children admired the building in the early 1900's, for it was the largest we had ever seen. It was fun to walk through the halls, and this we often did.

The steeple was not pigeon proof and when the droppings had built up to a depth of over a foot, the county court became fearful that the second story ceiling might give away. Finally, in June 1917, the court, consisting of Cadar Coats, presiding judge, George Isenhower of the eastern district, and A.W. Baker of the western ordered the removal of the steeple.

Captain Arch Frow of the National Guard, apparently at the request of the court, detailed four of his men to help a local carpenter, Karl W. Reiley, remove the steeple. The four men were Guy Ross, Cecil "Dart" Dryden, Arthur Lockwood and Doug Inglish. Guy Ross told me they slept in the courthouse and ate their meals at a north side cafe the two weeks they worked.

As the steeple was torn down, the lumber was lowered by ropes on the north side and then was hauled away by Ed Behymer, a local drayman.

Many citizens were opposed to the removal and put up quite a fight, according to Guy. They felt someway could have been devised to keep the pigeons out. After it was done, some said that the handsome appearance was greatly lessened and that it made for a squatty look.

Because of this major change and the removal and selling of one of the iron spiral stairs, our courthouse can never be placed on the National Register of Historic Buildings.

Some years later, we had a county court who didn't think it necessary to keep the building in good so many come and go these 100 years! Yes, in 1989, that majestic building standing there in the middle of our court yard will have a birthday. 100, if you please!

It is our hope that "she" will be gracing our downtown and serving all the citizens of Barton County for another hundred years and longer.

Courthouse, Lamar, Mo.

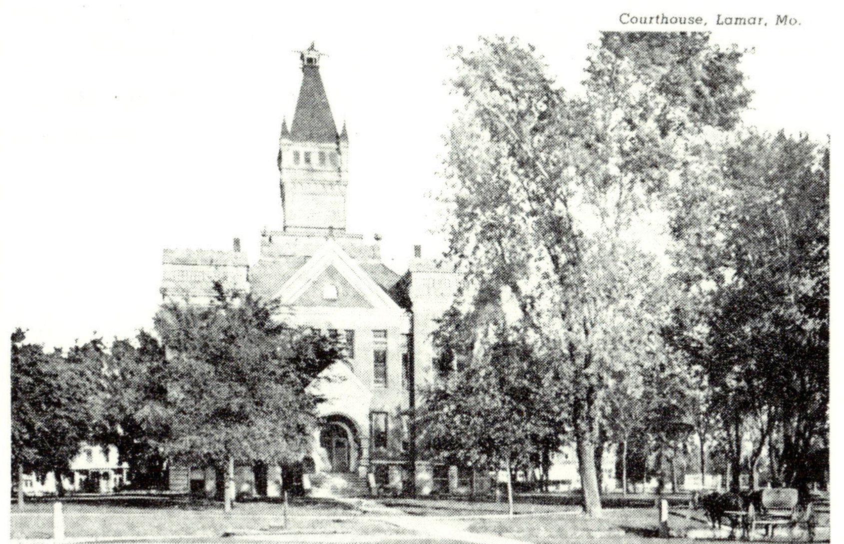

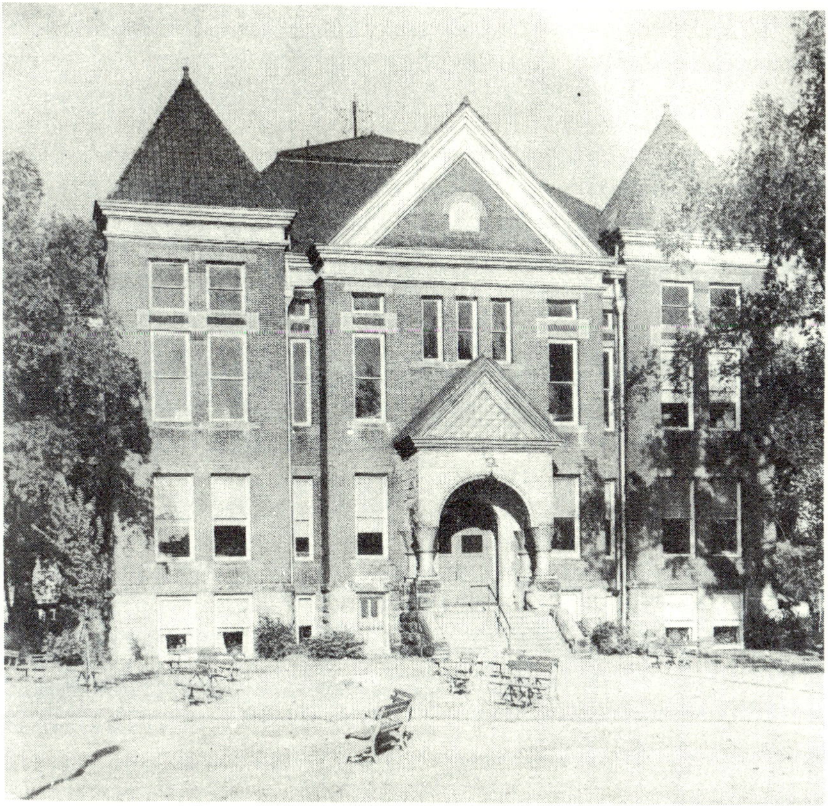

As the Courthouse Looks Today, August 1988

The Old, Wooden Icebox

August 11, 1988

The other day when I opened my refrigerator door, a picture of the old wooden ice box we had at home, when I was growing up, flashed into my mind. I have no idea why I suddenly thought of it.

I believe most of these boxes were made of oak and somewhere between four and five feet tall, depending on whether they were top or front loaders. They were metal lined, and as I recall, had only two shelves, so they didn't hold much food.

It was such an improvement over putting the milk and butter into a bucket or kettle and lowering it a ways into the cool well, that we were truly happy when we got one. We had no problem in the winter as the houses weren't furnace heated, not many anyway. If the kitchen was a little too warm, we put the food in some other room where is was really cold. Some people had cellars that were always cool. Besides putting the milk and butter down there, they also stored eggs, root vegetables from the garden, apples and the canned fruits, vegetables, jellies, etc. We children enjoyed sitting down there awhile to cool off when we were visiting where they had one.

There was one feature about the wooden ice box that we considered quite an inconvenience. The water from the melted ice had to go somewhere, so the inventor provided for this by constructing the ice compartment in such a way that the water drained through a pipe in the back part. This meant there had to be a pan on the floor placed in the right position to catch this water. The pan had to be emptied several times a day and the last thing before going to bed. That task fell to us girls and woe unto us if we let it overflow!

We had a square, red card with black numbers on it, designating pounds which we put up in the front window to tell the ice man how many pounds we needed that day. In the earlier days, the deliveries were by horse and wagon. Later, Model T Ford trucks were used and still later, Model A Fords.

The ice man carried the big chunk of ice with what I thought were huge tongs. These always fascinated me for I didn't understand how they held the ice. I was always sure it would fall, but it never did.

Jess Tucker was usually our delivery man and we girls looked forward to his coming, for he was kind to us and made us laugh with his funny remarks. We knew when he chipped the ice so it would fit into the box, that he would manage to have some good sized pieces for us. It was sheer heaven to have a piece to suck on until it melted! If it was too large to get into the mouth, we'd wrap a small piece of cloth or paper over the end to keep our fingers from "freezing."

Every household had an ice pick or two so we could chip ice for lemonade or cold water. We still have the one we started housekeeping with and it often comes in handy. We were married a number of years before electric refrigerators appeared, so our old pick has seen a lot of use.

It didn't occur to me when growing up to wonder where ice came from. As I grew older, I learned there was an ice plant down by the "Y" on the north side of the Frisco tracks (now Burlington) and both Tommy Tucker and Hattie Spradling told me that Guy Quackenbush made all the ice for years using the water from a deep well located nearby.

I have not been able to learn when this ice plant was built nor by whom. I do know that Albert Matthews brother of Mrs. Spradlings mother, Harriet Orahood, was an owner at one time. And by the way, he is the man responsible for bringing the much respected Negro cab driver, Jim Webb, to our town. But more about this later.

A Jack Kitner owned the plant for years and for some time was in partnership with "Heavy" Griffin, who also made and sold O'Joy pop. Harry and Paul Spradling bought it from Mr. Kitner in the early 1930's and in 1945, Paul and his wife, Hattie, who were now sole owners, moved the business to 1107 Cherry and called it, Lamar Ice and Cold Storage Company. Hattie continued to operate the plant after Paul's death selling it in 1965.

It has been difficult to learn who worked at the old plant through the years. Ruth Laycox Anderson said her late husband, Frank, was employed there for several years, but she doesn't recall who owned it at the time. Then besides Jess Tucker, an employee for 25 years or so, his son Tommy worked there for some time as did Red Dalton and Cecil Smith. Then there was Fred Peebles, who delivered the ice on just Broadway and Gulf street. He still used a horse drawn wagon, while the others were driving the early Ford trucks. I'd almost wager, he preferred it this way.

Eventually someone developed and all metal box which held 100 pounds of ice. It was called a coolerator and most of the more prosperous disposed of their wooden boxes to buy one of these.

And then came the electric refrigerators - somewhat crude by today's standards, I remember they had to be worked on a lot.

Most people were glad to dispose of the old wooden box, though some did survive by being put somewhere out of the way.

These are now being sought by home owners who want to decorate in the popular country style. They are handy for storage of barbecue equipment, picnic supplies, old recipe books, canned goods or whatever else your fancy dictates. Plan to pay a big price, or you won't get one!

This is the story of the wooden ice boxes and the ice that cooled them. What a welcome innovation they were back in the early 1900's! How glad I am, though, that we don't have to use them today!

Looking Back At 1919

November 19, 1988

Recently, a great-granddaughter of ours, who is attending SMSU at Springfield, asked if she could interview me for one of her class assignments.

The students were to talk with one of their eldest living relatives about the year that person was 18 years old, describing what life was like then for a late teenager and also what outstanding events took place in our nation that year. Since I was 18 in 1919, that was the year for me to describe and the following remarks are answers I gave to her questions.

We young people had many, many good times that year, just as our seniors do today - though I daresay in a quite different way. We had very little money, so we made our own fun, which of necessity couldn't cost much.

The junior class always entertained the seniors with a party and also the seniors put on a play in the Opera House, which always drew capacity crowds. There were get-togethers in the homes, as well as many church sponsored parties.

We had picnics out at the North Dam, hay rides on a frame pulled by horses, skating, Valentine and Halloween parties, to name a few. The last mentioned always included a scary visit to the old haunted house that stood near 11th and Oak. Most of our parties were chaperoned and we didn't mind at all, for the adults entered right into the merriment.

We liked to go in groups for that was more fun. My sisters and I quite often dated together since there were four of us.

Sometimes there were buggy rides into the country with the boyfriend of the moment. After cars came along, a bunch would go for a ride on Sunday afternoon, providing the roads weren't muddy, (no gravel or black top roads then.)

About once a week, several couples would manage to get enough money together to go to the Bijou, our only movie theater, owned and operated by E.E. Wagner. The price then was 10 cents for adults, 5 cents for children and one cent war tax on each ticket. Remember, a dime was as hard to get then as a $10 bill is now, or maybe harder.

We always went to one of the two bakeries after the show for a sundae, a soda, a limeade or a cherry phosphate.

We young people flocked to town every Saturday night for the band concert in the court yard. The Victrola was our other main means of hearing the popular music of the day. There were still some pump organs around and the player piano came in about this time, but in 1919 not many had one.

Some of the popular songs were "Missouri Waltz," "Tip Toe Through The Tulips," "Dardanella," "Three O'clock In The Morning," "I'm Forever Blowing Bubbles," and "Over There," which was a very popular war song.

In 1919, we didn't have very many changes of outer clothing. The few dress up ones were made either of wool for winter wear or silk, taffeta and linen. Mother or a hired seamstress made our clothes, for there were no ready-to-wear shops those days.

Silk hose hadn't been in very long, but most of us girls managed to have one or two good pairs of black ones. We wore black cotton or lisle hose to school, though.

By this time, most of us were wearing corsets with stiff staves which had supporters to hold up our hose. When not wearing a corset, we held up our hose with elastic garters just above the knees. They did the job but must have been hard on the circulation. No shaggy hair, faded or ragged garments were allowed, for we pupils were expected to look neat and clean at all times.

We girls took great pride in our long hair. I remember so well the fad was to wear smallish rolls of hair over the ears. These rolls, or "rats" were made of hair combings and were covered over with our real hair.

Some of us wore a big ribbon bow at the back of the head just above the neck, though one classmate, Alberta Snorgrass (now Wirts) insisted on wearing hers higher up. We must have looked freakish, but we thought we were right in style.

Our teachers were strict and we knew we'd better have our lesson or the whole class would have to take it over the next day. Seldom was there a serious discipline problem, but if something came up the teacher couldn't handle, the offending student went to the superintendent's office where he or she received the proper punishment. This was embarrassing and no one looked forward to going to the office.

Sports were not stressed as they are today - though we had both a track and a football team. We senior girls made sure we stayed after school to watch them for they were our heroes.

The main emphasis those days was on our studies - the 3 R's, so to speak.

Children were expected to help in the home. We sisters took turns with the dishes and shared the housework, gardening, etc. There were two chores I hated. One was keeping the water bucket filled from the well in the backyard and the other was making sure the coal buckets never got empty. This last was such a dirty task and that coal was so heavy!

It wasn't nearly so easy to keep up with the latest news in 1919, as it is today. The only newspaper many took was the Daily Democrat and Mr. Aull did his best to keep us informed on the news, especially the local. Not much happened that he didn't get into his paper.

The rural party lines helped the country people get the news. If someone heard something interesting, he or she (mainly she) gave one long ring and everyone hearing it knew to remove their receiver and listen.

1919 was an exciting year as "the war to end all wars," or so they said, ended on November 11, 1918,where an Armistice was signed. Boys were beginning to return from Europe and this meant meeting the trains with the band, having exciting parades, big dinners in their honor and social gatherings to celebrate their safe return. Some of our boys lie in Flanders Field and for their families this was a heart breaking time.

Another highly emotional event of this year was the mob hanging of Jay Lynch, who in early March had shot down both the popular sheriff John Harlow and his son Dick.

The trial was being held in the courtroom upstairs on May 28, and during the noon recess, the mob rushed up the stairs, forced their way into the small south room where he was, put a rope around his neck, dragged him downstairs, out the north doors and strung him up to a tree. There was a huge crowd, as word went out on the party lines there might be a hanging. I watched the whole thing - but then I was 18!

This was an important year in my life in more ways then one. Our graduation exercises were held in the Opera House the evening of May 16. We were the first class in Lamar to wear caps and gowns for graduation.

During that summer, I started dating Charles, who had just returned from two years service in France during World War I. We girls vied with each other to see who could get a date with a returned soldier or sailor. Sometimes, we had two "on the string" (1919 slang) and often found ourselves in a quandary as to which to date and which one to turn down.

And then, this was my first year of teaching in a rural school and a lifetime ambition finally reached. So, in September I was the teacher at Doylesport School in northeast Barton County at $50 per month and what a happy year that was!

1919 was also an important year in our nation's history. Besides having to adjust to the war's end, which was no small chore, Amendment 18 to our Constitution was passed by Congress. This was the Prohibition Amendment and it was ratified on January 16, 1919.

The 20th or Suffrage Amendment, was not actually passed until 1920, but much of the actual work on it was done in 1919. This one gave women the right to vote and Lucretia VanPelt now a patient at Lakeview, was the first woman in the county to cast her ballot.

One of our former great presidents, Theodore Roosevelt, died at his home, Sagamore Hill, Oyster Bay, New York on January 6, 1919. Woodrow Wilson was our President in 1991, serving from March 4, 1913 to March 4, 1921.

This is just a part of what life was like here in 1919, as seen through the eyes of a late teenager and the way I answered my great granddaughter, Trini Lachnit's, questions during the interview.

Suppose she'll make a good grade?

Area Life Before Electricity

January 28, 1989

So many of you have asked, and are still asking, what kind of grade our great-granddaughter made on her paper at SMS written after she interviewed me concerning the year I was 18 (1919). I am happy to tell you that she made an A.

Now, let us take a look at what life was like here before electricity was in common use in our homes. True, we had the first electric and arc lights here as early as 1887, but not many homes were wired until several years later.

I recall so well how happy we children were when we were finally able to have our house wired. We really thought it was something to turn on a wall switch in the living room and have it flooded with light. It likely was only a 60 watt bulb, but it was such a change from the dim light of a kerosene (coal oil) lamp that it did seem mighty bright.

Our first lights were just drop cords with a light bulb on the end. To turn on the light in the bedrooms and kitchen, we had to pull a chain which hung from the socket just above the bulb. It was so frustrating to go into a dark room and have to grope and grope for that chain!

Before we had electricity, most housewives did their washing on the board. However, some were lucky and had a wooden machine which was either turned by hand or powered by a gasoline motor. These made wash day easier. Both washing and then ironing with those heavy flat irons heated on the kitchen range were such hot tasks in the summer, as was the canning of the garden produce. How she would have appreciated and electric fan, but then, there was no such thing!

Sometimes, we had to eat our evening meal by lamp light and I assure you, we couldn't see too clearly what we were eating, unless we were close to the lamp. Young people today would find it hard to imagine what it was like to do our evening homework by the dim light of these lamps. Leita Smith Boas recalls that they had a Coleman lamp which was placed in the middle of the table around which the children did their studying. These lamps had two mantles and used gasoline instead of kerosene, resulting in a much brighter light.

The country schools and churches had wall bracket lamps with reflectors which people thought provided plenty of light for the evening box suppers, literary clubs and other entertainments, as well as for the church services on Sunday evening and prayer meetings on Wednesday night.

at night. They often came in handy on dark nights when the moon wasn't out, and it was time to make the nightly trips to the outhouse before going to bed.

It was our task to clean the chimneys every morning. We first washed them in warm soap suds, rinsed them well and then dried them inside and out with wadded up newspapers. That is what became of many of our Daily Democrats.

Without electricity, we had no sweepers. I have a vivid memory of my mother putting us to bed, and then sweeping the rag carpet in the living room with a broom. Women wore dust caps for this chore, as there was a lot of dust and they needed to protect their long hair.

In order to serve mashed potatoes, someone had to mash them well with a heavy wire masher and then whip them with a large spoon. Imagine, if you can, having to mix all cakes by hand. No housewife every dreamed she would some day be able to buy cake mixes which would require only a few moments of beating, and with an electric mixer at that.

Our coffee was boiled in a enameled pot. Both my grandmothers put egg shells in the pot while it was brewing. I never knew why, but I do know they made good coffee.

Even though we grew up in this period, we like occasionally to light one of the several lamps we have around, then turn off the electric lights and watch TV in the dim but soft light. More than once, we've resorted to our old lamps when the electricity went off.

All of this reminds me of the time in the early 1960's when the Antique Club came out to our newly restored old rock house, two miles north on Highway 71, for the annual Christmas party. To make the evening more authentic in the old house, we relied on our kerosene lamps and the candle chandelier in the dining room for our lighting. After we had eaten and were assembled in the living room for our gift exchange, I slipped upstairs via the kitchen stairs, put on an old long white muslin night gown like my grandmothers wore and a lace decorated night cap Edith Klein's mother made for me. Then I came down the front stairway at the south end of the living room in my stocking feet carrying a brass chamber stick with a lighted candle. I wish you could have seen the shocked expressions, as they saw me. I'm sure that for an instant they thought they were seeing a ghost!

Now you know what it was like before electricity was in general use in our homes. Since one doesn't miss what he has never had, we weren't aware of the inconveniences of that day. I suspect the younger generation, 50 to 75 years from now, will be feeling sorry for us today and wondering how we ever got along without the new gadgets they have.

A Little Known Story

February 18, 1989

Since President Lincoln's birthday was last Sunday, and since we'll be celebrating Presidents' Day next Monday, the 20th; it seems an appropriate time to tell you a little known story about Mr. Lincoln and his Gettysburg Address as related in a 1908 book, "The Perfect Tribute" by Mary R.S. Andrews.

The story begins on the mild, fall morning of November 18th, 1863 when a special train left Washington carrying a distinguished group of Government dignitaries, foreign diplomats and the Marine band from the Navy yard. In the midst towered a man seemingly preoccupied, awkward and ill dressed. He was Abraham Lincoln, the 16th president of the United States and he was journeying with his party to assist next day in the consecration of 17 acres at Gettysburg, which had been set aside as a final resting place for the men who fell there.

He had yet to write his speech and he was worried, for he felt so inadequate as compared to the main orator, Edward Everett. He knew Mr. Everett would deliver a polished speech, for he was an educated man who had served as Ambassador to England and was a former Secretary of State. He, also, had been a Senator and the Governor of Massachusetts.

After finding a stub of a pencil in a pocket and using a piece of wrapping paper Mr. Seward, his Secretary of State, had dropped in the aisle when unwrapping some books, he began to write. He rewrote the speech several times, cutting here and there or rearranging the sentences. Finally, he read the speech over again and was so disgusted he dropped it to the floor and stared out the window for some time. Later, he picked it up, folded it carefully and put it in his pocket. He was ashamed of it, but it was the best he could do.

At 11 o'clock the next morning, November 19, 1863, a huge crowd of about 15,000 gathered. As expected, Mr. Everett gave a 2 and 1/4 hour polished address in his clear, cultivated voice. When he sat down, there was a long storm of applause, cheering and clapping again and again.

Next, a tall 6 foot four inch gaunt figure rose and slouched across the open space and stood facing his audience. This was the President and every ear was strained to catch the first sound of his voice. Suddenly it came in a queer, squeaky falsetto. This then, high sound from such a huge body was too much, and a suppressed giggle went through the crowd. After a few words, his voice and tone gathered volume and the people seemed to stop breathing for fear they would miss a word.

His speech lasted only 2 1/2 minutes. There was no sound from the people. He stared at them a minute with his sad eyes. Not one hand was raised in applause. Slowly the big awkward man slouched back across the platform and sank into his seat. There was still no applause. His speech, as he feared, was a failure. The Marine band played a dirge; his part was over and he had failed!

Mr. Everett and others tried to congratulate him, but the President always stopped then by saying, "We'll not talk about my speech!"

At four o'clock the next afternoon, he decided to leave his desk and go for a walk. He was still suffering from the chagrin of his failure. "It must have been pretty poor stuff," he said half aloud. His long strides had taken him to the outskirts of Washington, when suddenly, a lad of about 15 came rushing through the hedge, tripped and but for Mr. Lincoln, would have taken a nasty tumble.

When the President asked what was wrong, he said. "Wrong, everything is wrong!" Then he went into a mad tirade against the Government and the President and said his brother, Captain Carter Hampton Blair of the Confederate Army, was dying in the prison hospital and had set him for a lawyer, so he could make his will. Mr. Lincoln assured him he was a lawyer of sorts and that he could write the will, so the two rushed to the hospital. "I can get you in for they know me here," said the lad. In his rushing ahead, he failed to see the guards salute the President.

When the will was finished, he told the wounded man his name was Lincoln and naturally the Captain asked if he was related to the President. "There's a sort of connection," the President replied. Next, he asked if he had read the speech in the newspaper that the President made yesterday, to which Mr. Lincoln said he hadn't

Still wishing to talk, he told his visitor that Senator Warrington who heard the speech at Gettysburg, had informed their sister it was one of the great speeches of history and that the speech so went home to the hearts of everyone that it would have been sacrilege to applaud it---that one might as well applaud the Lord's Prayer. It seems to me, an enemy, the dying soldier said, "that it was the most perfect tribute ever paid by any people to a speaker and I predict school children will be learning this speech 50 years from now."

The young brother saw the tears in Mr.. Lincoln's eyes, but the dying soldier didn't notice.

Then the 15 year old read the speech aloud and the young officer said, "I wish I could put my hand in the President's, for I admire him very much, even if we are enemies!"

Suddenly, a mortal pain struck as he held the hand of his new found friend in a torturing grip. The struggle ceased while his head rested in his brother's arms and his hand lay quiet where he had wished to place it--in the hand of the President, though he never knew he'd gotten his wish.

Don't you wish Mr. Lincoln could know the place his Gettysburg address has in our Nation's history.

Styles Of Yesteryear Recalled

April 8, 1989

Never again will I laugh at the style prominent when I was growing up, for they were a credit to the latest I saw on the Today show a few mornings back. I have never before seen such outlandish outfits as those girls wore!

The ladies of yester-year wore kimonos during their leisure, instead of the robes or brunch coats we wear today. These were made of large flowered crinkle crepe and resembled those. the Japanese ladies wore.

For everyday wear, mother hubbard dresses were popular. They hung loose from the shoulders, always had long sleeves and were seldom worn with belts. They were usually made of calico, as it was inexpensive, wore well and didn't fade if given reasonable care. I remember both my grandmother and my mother wearing these. Usually they tied a long apron around the waist. Women were happy when Nelly Don in Kansas City began manufacturing house dresses - the very first. Soon they were the rage all over the country and the comfortable mother hubbard gradually disappeared.

The proper outfit for dress-up occasions was a dark wool skirt worn with what was called a waist. These were made of different weight material according to the season. Whether summer or winter, the waists were always high-necked and long sleeved, and were worn with a pretty broach at the neck - quite often a cameo. Because the skirts were so long, no one every saw their high topped laced or buttoned shoes unless the skirts were lifted when crossing a rain or mud puddle.

One of the ladies in our church often wore a waist made of green changeable taffeta, and also a large hat with some of the same for trimming. That taffeta fascinated me, for when she'd move a bit, it would change color. I thought I had never seen a prettier waist!

No lady would ever be caught out without her hat and gloves, in the summertime her gloves were always white. It was considered a disgrace to attend church or a funeral without the accessories. The hats were often quite large and Mr. E.E. Wagner, owner of the Bijou, would flash on the scene, "Ladies, please remove your hats" just before the movie was to begin. Hats didn't go out of style altogether until the early 1960's.

When I was a little girl, the hair was parted right down the middle front to back, and the long hair on each side was pulled back and tightly braided into what we called pig tails. Sometimes, we wore a ribbon tied part way down on each braid and other times, they were looped back up and tied with pretty bows. The boys sitting behind us girls delighted in yanking our braids and sometimes, couldn't resist dipping the end of the braid into the ink well on the desk top.

It finally became stylish to have our long hair hang in curls. This was accomplished by rolling it up on kid curlers, if we had them, and if not strips of paper or cotton cloth were used. This was a tribulation for sure, for it hurt to have the hair pulled so tightly when being rolled.

Eventually, someone invented a curling iron which could be heated by putting it in the chimney of a lighted kerosene lamp. Many times, the iron got too hot and the hair was singed - not a pleasant odor either!

Then beauty shops began to open and the ladies could get marcels which made a series of waves over the head. Before this, she wore her long straight hair in a tight bun at the nape of the neck. The next improvement was permanent wave machines and how well I remember those monstrous looking things with all the clamps and cords. We always feared we might get burned.

The middy blouse was considered high fashion when I was in high school. With it was worn a pleated skirt in varying degrees of length, depending on the age of the wearer, but always long enough to cover the black sateen bloomers underneath. With these blouses, we always wore either a red or a navy blue scarf.

For many years men's shirts were made with a collar band instead of attached collars as they have today. The earlier collars were of celluloid which was stiff and uncomfortable, and were fastened to the band with collar buttons. Later, when shirts were made with collars, the housewife starched them and the cuffs on the long sleeves so they were stiff as boards.

The well-dressed gentleman always wore nice cuff links, a gold stick pin in the necktie and carried a watch in a little pocket provided for it under the trouser waist band. And, oh yes, they wore spats, too. In case you don't know what these were, Webster describes them as a cloth or leather covering worn over the unstep and ankle.

Much later, bell bottom trousers were in style and still later, someone woke up and realized trousers didn't need cuffs at all. This was a welcome change for they were just dirt catchers anyway.

Boys wore knee length pants up into the 1930's. These were buckled just below the knees. Our son got his first pair of long trousers when he graduated from grade school in Kansas City.

Both men and boys wore billed caps and the men wore hats a lot, especially for dress up times.

All ages wore long cotton knit underwear in the winter for years and years since the houses weren't warm all over as they are today. We either had to walk places or ride in buggies or wagons and we certainly needed the protection this underwear gave us. This custom began disappearing in the early 1920's and we girls, especially, thought this a good riddance.

Many other styles, which I haven't mentioned, came and went such as the flapper era for women's clothes and the bobby socks period for school girls. I believe it was in the 1930's that every woman felt she had to have a Princess Eugenia hat.

Yes, I have seen many changes in the styles but so far I've never known any to be as ugly and far out as the ones I saw on TV recently. I have a feeling very few women will fall for them. Time will tell.

A Bit Of Smelly History

June 22, 1989

As I think back to my childhood, I realize a lot of things here in Lamar had their own special scents, some of which were pleasant while others weren't.The first one I think of is that coming from both the north and west side bakeries each morning. If you timed it just right, you could be near one or the other when the bread baked by "Fatty" Thompson of the west side or that of "Peanuts" Wilson of the other was just coming out of the big ovens. Oh what a heavenly smell!

Occasionally, mother didn't have time to bake bread at home, and one of us girls was sent to town for a loaf. I can picture, even yet, "Slim" Rutherford of the west side as he pulled enough white paper from the big roller at the end of the counter to wrap it. He tied it with a string that came off a roll resembling a beehive a bit and then invariable cut the string with his pocket knife. Sometimes, he didn't wrap it too well and we couldn't resist reaching in and pinching off a hunk, even though we knew we'd be scolded when we arrived home.

The cinnamon rolls were baked next and oh how good they smelled! By this time, the shop was full of people and it was difficult to squeeze inside.

I always liked to go into the big dry goods store owned by "Toss" Harkless and located where Fashion Crossroads is today, for it had its own distinct smell. There were bolts and bolts of all kinds of fabrics on the shelves, for all clothing worn by women and children was made at home or by a dress maker. Mr. Charles Dicks, the first tailor in Lamar, made the men's suits in his shop at the rear of his store.

Selby Jones had a shoe store on the west side for a time. There were rows and rows of all leather shoes. Yes, even the soles were leather and so much easier to walk on than the soles we find on shoes today. I call them thin boards, for they are stiff as boards and so prone to be slippery. This store had a smell all its own and I like to shop there. Mr. Jones was always so courteous. Leather shoes are as scarce as hen's teeth today, for most are made of plastic.

Another store I like to visit was the Johannes Hardware and Implement Company on the east side just north of the Rag Bag where the vacant space is now. The mingling of metal odors with that of the harness, saddles and other leather goods, produced an unusual but pleasing smell.

And how I did enjoy going into the A.K. Anderson, Sid Callison and York and Griffin grocery stores where I always got a strong whiff of those bins of apples and the banana stalks hanging from the ceiling. I don't believe the apples in the stores today have that same good smell. I wonder why. Even the big rounds of cheese on the counter, from which the grocer cut the amount the customer needed, added to the aroma of those early day grocery stores.

N.B. Elam had a somewhat different kind of store on the north side also, as the east part was a grocery store and the west side where Miss Ida Elam and Miss Jennie Henry presided, was stocked with corsets, shoes, laces, yard goods and other supplies ladies would purchase. This store did have a different smell; but it wasn't offensive.

Then, there was the butcher shop owned by Fred Elliott and Fred Cross, which I didn't really like to go into. The fresh pork and beef hanging all around had a smell I could hardly stand. Even the several inches of sawdust on the floor had that same odor. In the real cold weather, they always had rabbits hanging outside that were for sale, and I never liked having to pass them. Maybe this explains why I can't eat rabbit today.

Then there were the doctor's offices. I remember so well going to Dr. Craigs and to Dr. Stones. We knew we were at the right place before we went inside, for the mixture of peroxide, quinine, calomel, castor oil, turpentine and other medicinal odors was so pronounced it seemed to seep through the door. It was far from a pleasant smell and I always had the urge to turn and run, but I never did.

I know nothing of the school coat room here today, (we called them cloak rooms), but I do recall that damp or wet wool coats and hoods mixed with that of wet overshoes (we say galoshes, today), produced an unpleasant odor. I always dreaded my turn as cloakroom monitor, because of this.

Most every yard had a mock orange bush, a lilac bush or two as well as a honeysuckle vine clinging to the fence. We girls often took early evening walks while these were in bloom so we could fill our nostrils with their heavenly fragrance.

I wonder how many little girls, walking to Sunday School, undid all their good deeds of the week just past by stealing a few blooms to pin on their collars?

These are just some of the odors about town in the early 1900's of course, there are many I haven't mentioned.

I don't notice our shops having such pronounced odors today. Could it be because so many items are now pre-packaged, or is it because my sense of smell isn't as acute now as when I was young?

Out Doylesport Way
July 20, 1989

There is something about the thoughts of the old one room school that tugs at our heartstrings, especially if we ever attended one or had the privilege of teaching in some of them. Those beloved one room structures were once the foundation of public education and now hold a special place in our Nation's history. I am grateful that I did get to attend rural schools a few years as well as teach in two before the love bug bit me.

During the early summer of 1919, I applied at Doylesport, which is just a few miles northwest of Milford. Before I had time to apply at more than one other school, I was hired at a salary of $50 per month, which to me was a big sum.

Arrangements were made to board with the J.R. Irons family who lived on the farm adjacent to the school. This was most convenient for me.

The first Monday in September finally came and the 22 children began arriving, anxious to see the new teacher. The first to get there was Bertha Boles with her six year old brother, Elbert, in tow followed by Floyd and Cecil, both of whom were also younger than she. You will remember Floyd as Smokey. Their father, Ed, was a board member as was Mr. Irons. Then pretty little brown eyed Lora Ward arrived. Her father, Vernie, was the third board member

Next came Forest Waits, better known as Kelly, with Otis and Everett Williams and Alta and Glenna Welker. The older boys even took it upon themselves to keep both the water bucket and the coal hods filled at all times. That big cast iron stove used a lot of coal on winter days; the building was larger then most rural schools and so there was a big space to heat.

There was a long bench for the lunch buckets and a smaller one for the water pail near the door. The wraps hung on hooks at the other end of this wall.

My desk was at the opposite end of the room and in front of it was the recitation bench where the children sat when they came up for their class sessions. On the wall, back of my desk, was a long slate black board for use by both teacher and children. I sometimes think, even today, that I can hear the click and the screech of the chalk on that slate, especially when one of the pupils felt a bit mischievous.

We also had a small library, a big world globe and an upright metal stand for the heavy dictionary, all of which were well used that year.

During mid-morning and mid-afternoon recesses the children enjoyed playing games such as ring around the rosy and drop the handkerchief for the younger ones, tag, ante-over, baseball and marbles for the older ones. I sometimes went out to share the fun with them and often I hated to ring my brass hand bell calling them back to their studies for they were having such a good time.

I never knew when Mr. L.E. Brous, the County superintendent would walk in to check on me. He liked to come un-announced and see us teachers in action.

At the close of the term, the eighth grade pupils from nearby schools went to Milford and took the examination to see if they were ready to enter high school, mine passed with flying colors!

The board members asked me to return but Oakton offered me $80 per month and I couldn't turn that down.

During the school term, I heard no mention of where the school got its name, nor anything about the cemetery which has been in the news since the Optimist Club decided to clean it out. There have been no burials there for years and it has become a mess of briars, vines, weeds and trees of all sizes.

Recently, Nadine Walters, Edith Klein and I visited the cemetery and we were amazed at how much the club had accomplished. In fact, I was able to read the inscriptions on some 20 stones, much to my joy. The earliest burial dates we saw were 1871, 1872, and 1873, and the latest was 1915. The Optimist fellows certainly deserve a vote of thanks for taking on this difficult task.

The Doyle family was very prominent in this vicinity in the early days. In fact, both James and Granville with their families are listed in the 1870 U.S. Census for Barton County.

The next to get there was Arlene Shepherd. She was the only one to give me an affectionate greeting. Then there was Johnny Irons, the four Rodebush children, Howard, Johnny, Ollie and Frankie, the four Robinson children, Earl and Delbert followed by their two pretty cousins Opal and Elva, and lastly Orville Rector and Cyldia Wilson.

No teacher in Barton County could possibly have had a nicer group of pupils, for they were well behaved, eager to learn and anxious to please me, their new teacher, whom they called Miss Reba. We had no major discipline problems the eight months I was there.

James and John Doyles who set up a kind of stop over and camping place on his farm for the people traveling through the country. This was a main traveled road to points south, as such a rest-stop was badly needed for weary travelers. Since it was located on a Doyle farm, it soon became known as Doylesport.

Gerald Allumbaugh, a former resident of this area, wrote me that his grandfather Peter Allumbaugh once had a blacksmith shop less than one-fourth mile south of this Doyle home, but on the opposite side of the road.

The National Archives and Record's service in Washington D.C. states there was a Post Master's report from Doylesport in 1868. In an 1877 report, the Summit Post Master said it was the late Doylesport, as they did have a Post Office for several years, though no one knows where it was located.

Therefore, there was a school, a cemetery, a post office and a blacksmith shop beside Mr. Doyle's rest stop. I have never found mention of a store or a church, however.

The records do say that in 1872, this area which had been a part of Newton Township became Doylesport Township, another honor for the Doyle family.

On January 26, 1869, Granville and Lucy Doyle purchased 40 acres and it was at the northeast corner that one acre was set aside for a school building. This gives us reason to believe that it was this family of Doyles who gave the land for the first school. Since the cemetery is adjacent to the acre set aside for the school but on the west side of it, that land came from the same farm, as well.

Old school records mention that there were 20 school age children on February 13, 1869 and by April 8, 1871, there were 42, so the district was growing rapidly and making the need for a school building more acute. James Doyle was elected to serve on the very first school board in 1871. Besides James and Granville, there was a John W. Doyle who was also a taxpayer as well as prominent in school affairs. He served as a director in 1876 and 1877.

The first teacher mentioned in the old records was J.L. McComb, who taught the term of 1873 and 1874. He later became a doctor and practiced in the county and particularly in Lamar for many years. By the way, the school was never referred to as Doylesport until the October 16, 1874 school board minutes.

The first school building was used until 1885 when the board voted to move one-half mile east and one-half mile north to the property of J.W. Short. This second building was only used until 1892 when it was moved to Mr. Short's farm and made into a barn.

The third building was erected on the same spot during the

summer of 1892 by A.E. Clarkson and Co. and was large enough to seat 60 children. There were two front doors which was unusual. This is the building in which I taught the term of 1919-1920.

Not mentioned previously was John Franklin Doyle who married Miss Ida Bryan. This Miss Bryan was a sister to Rebecca Bryan, wife of Daniel Boone. This John was descendant of Granville and Lucy Doyle and thus a fore-father of Carolyn Sue Doyle of Tulsa and her sister, Clara Doyle Seele, Medford, Oregon, both of whom have been a great help in sifting out the various Doyles and their contributions to the Doylesport area. But for this family, the school, cemetery and township would have another name.

We do owe the Doyles and all the other early settlers a great debt of gratitude - no doubt about that.

Doylesport School
1919-1920

**Teacher -
Reba Earp**

Grandmother's Apron

October 5, 1989

A description of life in the early 1900's would not be complete without mention of the important place grandmother's apron had in her life.

She had two kinds, both of which tied around the waist with a pretty bow in the back and came very near to the hem-lime of her ankle length dress. One type was for everyday wear in doing her house and garden chores. These were usually made of calico, checked gingham and in later years from pretty feed sacks. The other kind was for Sunday use or when company came, and usually were made of dimity, batiste, fine muslin or linen. Many had a pretty hand embroidered design and always there was tatting, crocheting, or store bought lace along the hem bottom, as well as on the ends of the tie. The women sort of vied with each other to see who could make the prettiest aprons. I recall that my two grandmothers had some real pretty ones which they always wore to protect their dresses.

Today, like the horse and buggy, an apron like these is seldom seen. Some of us do wear a cobbler type one, especially when cooking. These in no way resemble the ones grandmothers wore, though I often hear women-usually the slack crow-say they don't even own an apron. Old fashioned me can hardly understand that!

Grandmother had many other uses for her aprons. When I was a child, people seldom had screens on their doors and windows. If the threshers or even other company were there for dinner, she would scare off the pesky flies, while they were eating, with flips of her apron.

Her apron was mighty handy for carrying in some wood chips, kindling or cobs to start quick fire in the cook stove. Many times I've seen my grandmothers carry in baby chicks, just hatched, to put them in a warm place by the stove. Often it served as a receptacle for the eggs, too, especially when she forgot to take the egg basket out to the hen house, and yes, it also carried in vegetables from the garden and fruit from the orchard.

She often used her apron for wiping a perspiring brow when standing in the hot kitchen ironing hour after hour and also, when she continued hoeing in the garden even though the boiling sun was telling her to quit.

When she saw company coming up the lane, she would give the table tops a quick swipe to remove the tell-tale dust always, when they left, she would wrap her arms in that long apron, especially if it was cool outside, while she stood on the porch bidding them farewell.

Kleenex was unheard of and I remember the faithful apron being used to wipe away a tear when bad news came from someone on the telephone. And yes, aprons were handy to steady tottering footsteps when that precious grandchild was learning to walk.

Perhaps, the most common use was for removing hot pans from the stove. Hot pads weren't known as they are today. My grandmother Earp always had a canary and before going to bed, she would drape her apron over the bird cage. I never knew whether it was to keep the bird warm, as the house got quite cold before morning, or if it was to keep it from singing in the middle of the night.

The white, fancy aprons didn't have so many uses. They did make the wearer feel a bit dressed up, however. When company came unexpectedly, she would quickly change to a white apron and run the comb through her hair a few times to be sure there were no tag ends.

I have a lovely white one trimmed in spider web crocheting which was made by Edith Klein and her mother, Maude Werts. A few times when entertaining a club here, I've tied it around my waist to do the serving. It was a conversation piece for sure!

I know there were other uses, but these are a few that come to mind as I sit here writing. Perhaps, you can list a few more as people did after the article about "local smells" was in the paper. So many called or wrote from afar to tell me of smells they remember that I'm tempted to write a sequel.

Lamar Mayors Reviewed From First One In 1870 Through 25 Years With Gilkey

November 4, 1989

Prior to 1870, Lamar was a village in the strictest sense and was under the direct supervision of the county court. In February 1870, the villagers asked to be incorporated and this was granted under the name "Inhabitants of Lamar." The court then appointed the first board of trustees, who in turn chose William B. Ryan, chairman, and Wyatt Earp as constable.

In April, the citizens held their very first real election. Wyatt's father, Nicholas Porter Earp, was one of the judges.

For 11 years a board of trustees with one member being chosen chairman managed the affairs of the village. His function was merely that of presiding officer of the board. N.F. McCutchen was the last to serve in this capacity.

In the spring of 1881, Dr. Charles Van Pelt had the distinction of being the first regularly elected mayor of Lamar. The term was two years only. He was the grandfather of Cuddy (Lee) Van Pelt, whom many of us remember.

There were two Dr. Van Pelts here at that time. The other was Dr. Isaac N. Van Pelt. This was confusing to the townspeople, so Dr. Charles, the mayor, was nicknamed "Short" and Dr. Isaac was called "Slim." Miss Ora Van Pelt was a descendant of the latter and again, many of us remember her well.

In 1883, Capt. A.G. Hall was elected mayor. He was Lamar's veteran marble tombstone and monument dealer for many years and much of his artistic workmanship decorates graves at our cemeteries today.

The third mayor was S.E. McVey, who lived in a big white house on North Gulf, somewhere in between Dr. Gerald Swearingen's office and the Double Play Sports shop. He resigned in 1886 and R.H. Schofield, a former Union veteran finished his term.

In 1887, the fifth mayor, Allen Warden was elected. He came to Barton County in 1875 and in the intervening years held several public offices.

T.W. Harkless (Toss) became the sixth mayor in 1889. He operated a fine dry goods store where Fashion Crossroads is now, and was a very popular business man. He hired me to clerk in his store the summer of 1920, so I had an opportunity to know him well.

In 1891, Mr. Warden was re-elected and in 1893, S.D. Cox, a retired Union soldier was chosen to serve for two years. Following his term, Mr. Harkless was again elected.

Then in 1897, my great uncle John M. Earp, became mayor. He had the agency for Adams Express Company at that time and later had a first class jewelry store at the southwest corner of the square.

C.Y. Trice, known as the "Land Advocate," served from 1899 to 1901. Helen Thorpe was his daughter. The family home for many years was where Lohmeyer-Konantz Funeral Home is today.

Dr. H.T. Wells, a dentist, and the first Missouri born one, became mayor in 1901. He was responsible for improving the light and water systems, the laying of brick sidewalks and the removal of the damaged trees around and in the courtyard.

Our 13th mayor was Thomas Egger, who was president of a bank by his name located where Pahlow and Pahlow now are. He was a big portly man with too soft a heart for his own good.

In 1905, E. Stanley Wilson defeated his Republican opponent, Mr. Egger. He was considered one of our better mayors up to that time. His daughter, Cora, was my seventh grade teacher and a strict one, too.

After Mr. Wilson's tenure, Banker Egger was re-elected and held the office 10 years or until 1917. That was the end of the two year rule.

Then in 1917, another banker, Charles B. Edwards, was elected and served until 1921.

This year, my uncle John Earp was re-elected serving until 1926.

Following him, Alderman C.A. Lockwood, father of Admiral Charles Lockwood, of world fame, was voted into office. For some reason, Mr. Lockwood only held the office one year.

He was followed by Orrin P. Combs in 1927, who held the office until 1934. His son, Selby, was another of our three famous admirals in World War II. Mr. Orrin Combs was the father in-law of Zetta May Combs, who married son Clyde.

After Mr.Comb's term, E.A. "Slim" Rutherford was elected and served until 1941. He was a popular mayor.

In 1941, Guy Ross was elected and served until 1947. I suspect he would say the major event of his term was when the huge crowd came to see and hear Harry Truman formally accept the nomination for Vice President under Franklin Roosevelt.

Following Mr. Ross in 1947 was G. Carrole Combs, the middle son of former mayor, Orrin Combs. He served until 1953.

At that time Loyd Gathman was voted mayor and he served until 1959. This was the period when Lamar was having serious water problems. Old muddy went dry and the water from "Old Stinkey," the city's deep well, wasn't fit to drink. (That was Madeline Aull's name for the well.) Even then, the townspeople twice voted down bonds to construct a lake!

Norbert Heim was elected in 1959 and served until 1965. He was the mayor when we restored the old rock house north 2 miles on Highway 71.

Lastly, Gerald Gilkey became mayor in 1965 and as of this date is still in office.

As I look back over this list of 25 mayors. I'm amazed to note that I remember all of them except Dr. Van Pelt, R.H. Schofield, Allen Warden and S.D. Cox. All the others, I remember seeing many times, not necessarily when they were mayor, for many lived a long time after serving.

We have been so fortunate to have had such high type men willing to serve our community in this way. The fine town we have today is the result of the excellent leadership.

My thanks to the girls at the City Hall for helping me with the later ones who served while we lived in Kansas City.

Earlier Christmases

Christmas 1989 is fast approaching and as I "make my shirt tail crack" decorating the house, buying and wrapping the gifts, writing the letters that go out with each Christmas card, baking goodies for the holidays, and going hither and yon to Christmas coffees and parties, I can't help but think about the way we celebrated the birth of our Christ when I was growing up. There wasn't much similarity to our celebrations today!

For instance, we didn't even have a Christmas tree in our home and very few did. The only time we ever saw one was when we attended Christmas Eve services at our church. It was decorated with handmade paper chains, both cranberry and popcorn strings and lastly small tin candle holders which were clipped on to the branches. At the right moment, the little red candles were lighted casting a soft glow about the room. Oh how beautiful that tree looked to our young eyes!

I wonder now how come we never had a fire due to the candles. The tree was fresh cut, so was green and not yet easy to burn. Stores didn't sell shipped in trees those days. If we had one at church, some of the men and big boys went to the woods and cut one for the occasion.

We children knew that before the evening was over Santa would enter the church with his ho! ho! and give each child a little sack holding a few pieces of colorful candy and also either an apple or an orange. We always hoped for an orange since we seldom got one.

We heard our first Christmas carols at this Christmas Eve service. The organist would play the old fashioned pump organ and everyone would join in the singing. Sometimes, we children spoke pieces about the Christ child and about Santa Claus. It was always a joyous evening for all of us children and one we looked forward to all year long. The church was always the center of our celebrating.

People didn't send out cards and letters as they do today. I suspect it was largely due to the fact the people we knew lived close by and weren't scattered all over the country as they are today.

Penny post cards were popular then. The Christmas ones always had a pretty scene on the front. Young girls of or near dating age often received one from a young man who "had his eyes on her," as we said then.

Children did not expect a lot of expensive toys as they do today. I shudder when I think about the cost of these and how careless many children are with them.

We children did well if we got two simple gifts and I might add we were happy with them. I recall the first Christmas after our farm home burned in 1908 when I received a cloth back story book and a little red doll chair. It didn't bother me at all because I didn't have a real doll to set in it, for my imaginary one would do just as well.

There was one Christmas when each of us four sisters got a real gold ring. I don't remember that we got anything else, but oh how we adored those rings! I lost mine when I was a teenager, but my sister Dode still has hers. We were on a church picnic out at Orndorf's Ford, east of town, and while some of us were playing around in the water, my ring slipped off my finger leaving me heart broken.

Eventually, Christmas Eve arrived and we girls had a hard time going to sleep. We had each hung one of our long black stockings on a chair post for Santa to use for our gifts. We always hoped we'd find an orange in the bottom of the stocking, but usually it was an apple, for they were easier to get.

There was one Christmas when I received a flimsy doll buggy which I just loved. The following summer, Ruby and I hitched the cat to the buggy with string. The minute we turned it loose, it made a dash for the small air opening in the foundation of the smoke house. That was the last of my doll buggy.

I don't remember that grown-ups exchanged gifts as we do today. In those days Christmas celebrations were mainly for children.

No one ever thought of putting a wreath on the front door; neither did we decorate our homes inside, as we do today. That didn't lessen the joy of this holy season one bit, nor did we mind getting only a few simple gifts. We were happy with what we did receive. We had never had a lot of toys and so, didn't expect them. We don't miss what we have never had. How different it is today!

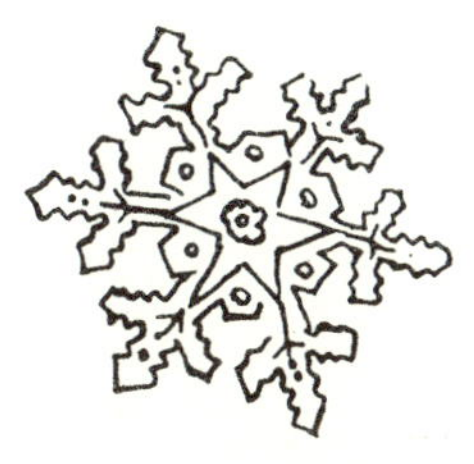

Butchering On The Farm Recalled

January 31, 1990

Lee Roy Dale suggested one day that I write an article about butchering. While we didn't live on a farm very many years, I do recall quite a lot; the rest of my information comes from hearing the family and friends talk about it in later years.

It was always done on a very cold, crisp winter day with several neighbors coming in to help. Water was heating in a big iron kettle in the yard, by the time the helpers arrived. The hog to be butchered had been fed carefully for months and the night before it was shut up and given no more food.

Two different methods were used to stun the animal which by now had been brought up near the scalding area. Some shot it between the eyes with a 22 caliber rifle and others knocked it in the head with the back part of an ax. In either case, the jugular vein was cut immediately while it was stunned and it was allowed to bleed well.

The hot water was transferred to either a wooden or steel barrel. Methods used for dunking the hog in this hot water also varied. Charles, my better half, says it was a job to dunk it just enough so the bristles weren't too hard to get off. Each man had a hog scraper and they worked quickly until the bristles were about all off, leaving a soft pinkish skin color.

It was next raised to a comfortable height for working. After letting it cool awhile, the carcass was split down the center of the belly, so the innards could be removed. The heart and liver were cut out first, put into a buck of cold water and saved until later. Part of the intestine was also saved to be used as a casing for the sausage. Now the hog was ready to be drawn up high and left until it was thoroughly cold.

The hard work really began after the cooling, for the carcass was placed on a table and it was cut and sawed down to the back bone, thus dividing it in half. The hams, shoulders and bacon were cut and trimmed and then hung in the smoke house over a slow burning hickory wood fire. Some women also liked to smoke the sausage. The thought of meat cured this way makes my mouth water yet today. If not smoked, the sausage was fried down, cooled, and then stored in the lard - yes, in the lard.

The back bones, spare ribs and tenderloin would keep awhile in a real cool place. Sparkie Robinson said her mother always prepared some of the liver for supper that night. It was a common practice to share this fresh meat with the helpers who in turn shared with them when they butchered.

The fat, that had been trimmed off, was cut up some and cooked outside in an iron kettle, Someone stirred it occasionally with a long wooden paddle to keep it from sticking. This melted grease was strained through a cloth; some people used the lard press to squeeze out the last bit of grease. The remains were called cracklings (we say cracklin's here) and if you've never eaten cracklin' corn bread, you haven't lived! The grease was poured into a big stone jar and set in a cold pantry. This process was called "rendering the lard." When my cousin, Betty Thiebaud, was a little girl she wanted something off a shelf in the pantry. So, she stepped up on the edge of the jar and started to reach up when she lost her balance and went right down into the lard. Can't you just imagine the scene that followed?

It was quite a task to clean the entrails inside and out so the sausage could be stuffed into it by means of the sausage press. They did this when they were planning to smoke it.

Would you believe the head was placed on a chopping block and cut open with an ax? First, the brains were removed and set aside in salt water. Mother always cooked ours for breakfast the next morning. No, I didn't eat any.

Usually the tongue was cleaned, cooked and then pickled as were the feet., The heart was usually baked with stuffing. The meaty bones were boiled and the meat on them was used for head cheese, which was truly delicious.

Sparkie also said her mother cleaned the paunch (stomach to me) thoroughly and filled it with certain vegetables and baked it. I asked if they ate the stomach and she said, "No, we ate only the contents, and they were good!"

The side meat was soaked in brine; could that be the same as the salt pork I buy today for cooking beans?

The scrap entrails were thrown into the hog lot and that mess soon disappeared.

Some say everything about the hog is used but the squeal; Sparkie said her father, Ollie Dumolt, told them he made whistles out of the squeal, so it wasn't wasted at their house.

And now the clean up! It seemed everything in the kitchen got greasy, even the door knobs, and that it took forever to get rid of it. There is a de-greaser on the market today, which makes the task much easier.

Think you might like to try butchering some time?

Oakton -- 1920

March 7, 1990

I had looked forward the entire summer of 1920 to the fall, when I would be going out to Oakton School to begin my year as their teacher. Oakton is four miles west and two south of Lamar, which meant I'd likely get to go home oftener on weekends than I had when at Doylesport.

The Sunday afternoon in early September finally arrived, and a friend took me and my trunk of belongings out to Grandma Perry's home where I was to board. She was the widow of Elias Washington Perry, whom everyone called "Wash." In later years, everyone called his widow Grandma Perry. Not once did I ever hear anyone say Affa Perry!

After leaving the trunk, we drove over to the school house to look it over. The yard looked so pretty with all the oak trees around and the building inside was so clean! The well-kept cemetery bordered the yard on the north. I learned later that the school house was built in 1895, though it didn't look 25 years old that day.

Monday morning finally arrived and so did the 30 children with their bright eyes, expectant smiles and clean shining faces. It was obvious they were wondering what I looked like, and also if they'd like me.

Most of the children had to walk quite a distance. However, Harold and Vernon Eales rode their Shetland ponies every day, keeping them in a small building on the grounds. Vernon told me recently that they often let the children ride during the lunch hour. One of the older boys, Paul Williams, really wanted to ride but the ponies wouldn't let him. For some reason, they disliked Paul and would invariably buck him off.

There were four of Charlie Perry's children - Floyd, Charles Jr., Dorothy and Marjory and five of the 10 Nathan Schlupp offspring - Noah, Esther, Waldemar, Lorene and Marie (later known as Jackie) Waldemar has been called "Dutch" for many years, and it was he who noticed my small diamond engagement ring the very first day I wore it on my finger. He asked what it meant. I also taught Mildred and George Thiebaud and George Diggs. Then there were Charles Jr. and Mary LaForce and Lora and Lida Blanchard.

I sometimes spent weekends with the Blanchard girls. One morning, we were trying to get on the other side of a creek by walking across on a dead tree. Naturally, they both went right along, but I lost may balance and stepped off into the water. Cecil

Blanchard and some of his friends were cutting wood and saw me step off. They thought it was funny to see the teacher get wet.

There were Paul and Lola Williams an a little cousin whose name I've forgotten, but who died that fall with the flu. He had a sister named LaVonne who was a pupil. Our school was closed a week, but so far as I can recall, no other children contracted it.

Then there were Dee and Joe McKibben. I remember how careful they were not to waste paper. Joe went on to be a doctor in California. Dee's son tried his best recently, to entice me to say his father, at times, was a problem at school. He had no   luck, though.

Next, there were two Hagins children - Mildred and Lester, better known as "Bus." I often wrote playlets for the children to act out as learning experiences and I recall one time when Mildred got to be the Christ Child in the Christmas play. She has never forgotten that..

I could never forget the Delay children - Stella, Tressie, Ada and Leslie. Sometimes they had parties on Saturday evenings and we had a lot of fun playing parlor games. They had the first player piano I ever saw. One of their rolls was. *"I'm Forever Blowing Bubbles."* Someone would pump it and the rest would gather around and sing. And yes, there were two good looking older brothers, Frank and Virgel, but they didn't attend school - too old.

Four of the little ones started their formal education that year. These were George Thiebaud, Marie Schlupp, Mary LaForce and George Diggs.

Occasionally, we planned special programs for Friday after recess and invited the mothers. Then in warmer weather, we would take a hike during the noon hour down the road to the North Fork Creek which meandered along among the many trees. We always planned something specific to watch for and talk about later.

During the winter, we sometimes had literary debates on Friday night for the adults, and what crowds we did have! Two or three of the older boys would come to the Perry home and walk with me to the school and then back home again. They didn't like the idea of me walking alone past the old creamery, which had been vacant a number of years. It was sort of spooky and I appreciated the boys' thoughtfulness. These evenings usually ended with a pie supper.

I really hated to see the school year close, for it had been a nice one. The children were all so dear, and so eager to learn. Then, I had thoroughly enjoyed living with Grandma Perry and her daughter whom I called Aunt Kate, for they did so many kind things for me. I liked their little home which Mr. Perry had built after his marriage to Miss Affa Brown, daughter of Senator Robert E. Brown. It was located west of the store building and the creamery on a part of his farm. He came to that section some time after 1860, and it was on part of his farm that a lot of Oakton was built.

The parents and children planned a dinner on the last day of school. When I walked in that morning, there was a big black umbrella opened and hanging upside down near my desk. I could see it was holding something, but I had no idea what, until one of the pupils said after dinner, "Miss Reba, You'd better take your umbrella down, I believe there's going to be a shower. Miss Reba wasn't afraid of any shower, but she knew the youngsters had something up their sleeves, about that sunshade. So she proceeded to take it down. As she did so there was a mighty clattering and banging, as a cataract of tin and aluminum ware poured down upon the floor. The children had planned a surprise wedding shower of tinware, for I was to be married to Charles Young of Kansas City, on May 7th.

The kids had gotten the teacher a half a dozen tea spoons, two aluminum ladles, two cookie cutters, two dippers, a percolator, a tea strainer, a pudding pan, and lots of other tin and aluminum ware, as their parting gift. With each gift was an original verse, written by young donor. Would you believe I still use some of those tin pieces today?

I can't close this article without giving you a bit of the history of this nice little village. It was first named Oak Grove for obvious reasons. In 1898, the residents decided to rename it Oak Town and that later became Oakton. The village had its main growth in the 1880's.

It is believed that two brothers, Hiram and John McManis were the first business men in Oakton. First, they built a store at the intersection on the southeast corner about 1881. However, it burned after two years. Then Hiram secured a lot over on the southwest corner from Mr. Perry and Opened another store, while his brother and a James H. McMurphy constructed a blacksmith shop where the first store had been. Mr. McMurphy worked with Mr. McManis and later bought the shop.

In the meantime, a small addition was added to the store building on the north. This was to house the first post office at Oakton in 1898. Mr. McMurphy's daughter Grace, was the first rural carrier in the county, carrying it from Oakton to Lamar and back. Some think she was the first in the nation, though I don't believe it was ever proven.

In the intervening years, the store changed owners several times. Some of those were Will Berry, a Mr. Renner and Nathan Schlupp, who purchased it in 1906 from Billy Snook, a son-in-law of Mr. Renner. Mr. and Mrs. Claude Crockett were the last owners, closing up shop about 1964. Mr. Schlupp was the owner the year I taught out there. Other than the antiques Bill Schlupp had in the store for awhile, it has stood vacant - a sad reminder of by-gone days.

The cemetery, which even today is well maintained and pretty, was established on a part of Mr. "Wash" Perry's farm, also. It is still registered as Oak Grove Cemetery.

The Methodist Church, a wooden structure, was built in 1894 and was just across the road east from the cemetery. George Diggs told me that in 1948, the church people decided it was time to have a new, modern building and so, the men rolled up their sleeves and removed this early building. Charlie Suiter acted as supervisor and each man in the church did his share of the actual building. By all working together and planning well, they were able to complete the new brick building in 1949. It is this church's present membership that presents the annual Christmas pageant which draws crowds from far and near to see this outstanding, outdoor reenactment of the birth of Christ.

In 1895, the Baptist Church was built just north of the cemetery. In the 1970's it was taken down and the lumber given to the Iantha Baptist Church. This land reverted to the Charlie Perry children and they, in turn, presented it to the cemetery association, according to Bob Perry.

All thought the years, the settlement had a village smithy who operated the blacksmith shop. When I was at Oakton, the smithy was a large, stocky man by the name of John Brigger. He lived next door with his sister, Mrs. Van Dorn, and her three children, Hazel, Edna and Harry. He definitely was an important part of the village history, just as the store was the hub of the community.

In 1902, a large group of Swiss Germans immigrated to this community from Iowa and Illinois. They were dairy farmers and owned creameries back there. C.F. Banwart, Ed Thiebaud and Nathan Schlupp were stockholders as well as office holders while it was in operation. E.L. Banwart actually did the operating of the business. They made butter and cheese and did well at first. And then margarine, a butter substitute, was put on the market and that spelled doom for the creamery. I don't know just when it closed, but I do know it had been closed several years when I went out there to teach in 1920.

I do want to add that on the northeast corner of the intersection when going into Oakton, there stood a big, white two story house that looked like a mansion to me. I finally learned it belonged to Lewis and Minnie Rudisaile, the parents of one of my favorite teachers, Matie Rudisaile Veale.

And so ends the story of a once thriving little village inhabited with some of the finest people in the world. But, like as many others, cars and good roads ruined the business in these small villages as people went elsewhere to shop. Eventually, I suppose, most will be gone forever.

I could not have written the history part of this article without the help of Bob Perry, who had given it as a program for the Historical Society some time back. Then, too, George and Helen Diggs, Mildred Hagins Zulian, Vernon Eales, Mary Lisher, Claudine Crockett, George Thiebaud and Mildred Thiebaud Sutherland came through with information when I was a bit hazy on some things. Without their help, I could not have written the true story of this once bustling, little settlement.

Remembering Andy Baker

April 4, 1990

Lately, several have asked me to write some articles about people who lived here when I was growing up. Almost the first person to pop into my mind was Andy Baker, who was in the grocery business here for several years.

He was very popular around the square, as well as with the townspeople as a whole. To know Andy was to like him. He was the type of man whom you never forgot, once you made his acquaintance.

He was a native Barton Countian, having been born on December 25, 1865, in the extreme northern part of our county near where the little village of Wise once stood. In 1893, he married Miss Jennie Lloyd.

Eventually, they found themselves at Jasper, where Dean was born June 16, 1908. Some of you may remember how Dean got the nickname of Cannon Ball, which stayed with him all his life. In writing up the account of a school game he had just seen, Arthur Aull said in his usual, colorful way, "The ball that Dean Baker threw literally flew across the field like a cannon ball. "That was all the kids needed to start calling him that and it stuck.

The next child, Ruth, was also born in Jasper on April 5, 1910. She passed away just about three years ago.

The family then moved to Lamar where the last child, Ann, was born on December 11, 1912. Mr. Baker opened a grocery store just off the northwest corner of the square on Gulf, where a tavern is now located.

He soon needed more room, so he moved to the east side of the square in about the middle of the block, using two store spaces, which made his the largest grocery store here at that time.

Meredith Dubin, Carl Riley, Bivon Earp and Clinton Goss were clerks. Ruth and Ann took care of the candy and tobacco counter and also candled eggs brought in by the farmers. Dean was the delivery boy and the father, Andy, took care of the meat counter. Mrs. Baker was the cashier.

The third store was on the south side in about the middle of the block where Galloway's Clothing Company had been located, and his last one was on the west side near where Bob Potter's Mens Store now is.

Andy was very popular with the children. Often they would go into the store and ask him if he had any scrap candy. Being so kind hearted, he would put a few pieces in a little brown sack and give it to them.

Pauline Jones Cooper wrote me all the way from Joshua Tree,

California, to tell me of a valuable lesson he taught her when a child. Her mother had sent her to his store to buy some cookies which were in a barrel. While she was putting some in a sack to be weighed, she ate a couple or so. Andy didn't say a word, but after he had weighed them, he took out the number she had eaten and explained that those were for the cookies she had eaten. She ended by saying she never again sampled food in a store.

Johnny Wagaman told me of one time when he and Keith Bartlett were just youngsters. They decided they'd like to try smoking. so they pooled their pennies and went into the store and asked for a package of "Twenty Grand" cigarettes which cost 11 cents a pack. When they were questioned, one said he was getting them for his father. They went to Johnny's garage and each lit a cigarette. Being a rainy day, the air was heavy and instead of the smoke rising it seeped out through the cracks. Mrs. Wagaman saw the smoke and rushed out. She sent Keith home on the run and you might ask Johnny what happened to him after that!

Andy was quite an entertainer and kept his guitar and harmonica at the store. He wore a heavy wire around his neck to hold the harmonica in place, so he could play both it and his guitar at the same time. He loved to sing and often tap danced for his

customers. He had a favorite reply, according to Ruby Weidman and her sister Alvira Glaze, when someone asked for something he didn't have. He always said, "No, I'm out, but I have plenty of prunes!"

The youngest daughter, Ann , had a pet dog she called Towser. One day, it ran out to Mayor John Earp's car, got caught under the wheel and was killed. In her grief and rage, she fixed a big placard denouncing him for running over Towser. She put this in her father's store window for all to see.

In a few days, in came the mayor carrying a snow white spitz puppy to replace her pet. Of course, she was overjoyed! She named the new puppy Snoodles, tied a pink ribbon around his neck and carried him almost everywhere she went.

In those days, people sometimes had narrow escapes just as they do today. One day Mrs. Baker and her sister, Miss Edna Lloyd, were driving down a hill on their way to Milo. Something scared the horse and it ran at full speed. One line broke, so they had no control. Just as they came to a bridge in a hollow, one yelled, "Whoa!" and the horse stopped. The dashboard broke off, their two little dogs were pitched out with the sudden stop and the two women were scared half to death - but unhurt.

Andy had such a big heart and just couldn't refuse when someone asked for credit. Too many failed to pay him later and the debts mounted until he was forced to take out bankruptcy. He worked for a while as a night clerk at the hotel and his wife, Jennie, was employed at Al Faubion's Laundry.

The family later moved to Atchison, Kansas, where they lived until he became ill. He died July 17, 1933, at Bronaugh where he is buried.

Ann is the only one left now of Andy's immediate family. Old-timers will remember her as that pretty little Anna Baker with the golden curls.

She has many demands on her time, for she is an accomplished pianist. At the moment, she plays for the residents at Baxter Manor Nursing Home as well as at her church. She also helps in the Humane Society Thrift Shop.

I am indebted to her for much of the family information and for the loan of the pictures.

Remembering Jim Webb, Our Popular Cab Driver

May 9, 1990

When I was growing up, we did have a handsome black cab river here whom everyone trusted and liked. He came to Lamar few years before 1900 and was a familiar sight on the streets of ur town for many years. He met every passenger train, rain or hine, that came through on both the Missouri Pacific and the 'risco, as they were called then. This was our chief mode of travel; /e even rode the trains to Kenoma, Golden City, Irwin, Sheldon nd Liberal.

I remember as well his first cab which was drawn by two iorses. Jim sat out in front and higher then the passengers. He olded his black slicker (we say raincoat) so he could sit on it. It ;uaranteed him protection if it began to rain, sleet or snow.

According to Charley Hylton, he kept his cab and horses in Mr. 3ert Matthews livery stable on Pacific Street (now called 10th) just >ff Broadway and on the north side of the street.

Charley also told me Jim had a small office up front and when inyone came in to order a cab he would ask them to write the nformation on the black board he had there. Then when Charley, or other fellows he knew came by he would have them read the messages to him until he had it all memorized. I'd wager he never once missed an appointment! You guessed it - Jim couldn't read or write.

When Charley, who worked at the First National Bank, discovered that Jim was carrying too much money around for it to be safe, he persuaded him to use the bank for his protection.

There was a school for black children at the southwest corner of 14th and Grand. Near the turn of the century, a Miss Mattie Tucker, also black, came here to teach. She and the good looking cab driver soon became fast friends and later were married. The family home was at the northwest corner of 14th and Walnut Streets, where Othal and May Gardner now live.

They had one daughter, Zella, who often begged to play with the neighborhood children. Her mother was sometimes overheard explaining to her why she couldn't; a sad experience for that little girl.

Zelda Metsinger's folks, Curly and Bess Hosselton, operated the Commercial Hotel where the *Democrat* is, for a good many years. Zelda told me her mother had a special table in the kitchen where he always ate. She said, too, that when she was a little girl she ate most of her meals right there with him.

John York, whom old timers remember, had a restaurant on the west side of Gulf Street between 9th and 10th. He, too, had a special place for Jim to eat, and Charley said he and other fellows often went back and ate with him. Everyone who knew Jim liked him and the color of his skin made no difference whatsoever. I'm certain the other restaurant owners were equally good to him.

Helen Shreves (now Massey) and her friend, Hazel Duncan, lived down by Kenoma and while in high school they went home every weekend on the 4 p.m. Frisco train. They received permission to skip study hall on Friday afternoon and took their suitcases to school that morning, so they would have time to walk to the depot to catch their train. Jim always managed to just happen by as they walked and he would take their suitcases to the depot free.

Docky Dimond can tell some interesting stories, too, about favors Jim did for him. No wonder everyone liked him!

According to Eldeva Griffin, her uncle, Floyd Selvey, and Jim were in business together for a time on Broadway - a couple doors north of the intersection. We evidently lived in Kansas City by then, as I have no memory of this.

My sister, Dode, just swears that her gang of friends called him "Uncle Jim," because he was so nice to them always.

Eventually, he gave up his horse drawn cab and bought a Model T Ford. According to Charley, he had a hard time learning to drive it because he had unusually large feet and the three pedals were so close together.

Mrs. Webb loved music and even taught it awhile. She continued her musical studies until her teacher died in 1918.

In 1918, she had the Asian Flu, as did most of us. However, she never fully recovered and the doctors said the flu left her with "leakage of the heart." Because she wanted to pass away in her home town of Independence, Kansas, Jim and the daughter took her back where she would die among her own people.

The Lamar Democrat had this to say about her when she died, "Mrs. Webb was held in high esteem for her quiet worthiness and her untimely death is a matter of deep regret to the people who for so many years have felt such kindly regard for her and her husband." Mr. Aull went on to say, "everyone in Lamar sympathizes with good old Jim in this loss. They know how lonesome he will be and their hearts go out to him." Wasn't that a nice tribute for a black family to receive?

In his later years, he went to Kansas City to live with his daughter, and the once familiar sight on our streets was gone forever.

There were a few other black families here during my growing up years. Perhaps the best known were Al and Belle Reed, who lived at the extreme end of West 10th Street. Belle did cleaning for the townswomen. She also helped with the cooking for dinners, parties, etc. Edith Klein reminded me she had worked for both Mrs. Judge B.G. Thurman and Mrs. John Earp. Al was the trashman and also cleaned the outdoor privies for the residents.

I believe they had a daughter Beulah, who also worked out and there was a son who often sang at the picture show when Stella Griffin was pianist. There was one song everyone liked that went something like this, "I'm tying the leaves so they won't come down and Nellie won't go away." Ever hear it?

Belle died before Al and later he married a woman with at least one son who made his living shining shoes at the corner barber shop. I think he was called "Happy."

Then there was Tom Gee who was a fine brick mason. He lived down by the Negro School and was about as broad as he was tall. He was a staunch friend of George Ward, grandson of our town's founder. No one dared say anything against him in Tom's presence.

I'm sure there were other black people here from time to time, but these are the ones I remember.

My thanks to the many who helped me recall various events and a very special thanks to Charley Hylton, for without his help, I couldn't have gotten this article together.

From Horseback to Jet Planes and Space Ships

July 11, 1990

During my lifetime, I have seen many changes and not one has been more obvious than our methods of transportation.

So far as I know, people had no way to get about at first except by horse-back or on foot. Would you believe that one branch of my family walked all the way from North Carolina through Tennessee to Bowling Green Kentucky? The few horses they had carried their belongings; the adults even took turns carrying live coals as there were no matches yet.

Then I remember hearing the family talk about my great-grandmother riding horse-back to church. I'm quite sure other women had to do the same.

My first memory of going a distance was riding in the old lumber wagon from Milford, where we lived, to Lamar. Two horses pulled the wagon. It was slow traveling, but we were used to it. There was a spring seat up front for mother and father, while we children sat in the back on a old quilt or comforter which had been spread over some hay or straw. It was rough riding, for the roads were full of ruts. No one had yet thought of smoothing the ruts and spreading gravel.

I was always afraid to cross the old City View Bridge in the heavy wagon for I feared the floor boards would give way and into Muddy Creek we'd go! Even today, I don't like to drive over the new bridge that replaced the old iron one.

Eventually, we got a buggy which was quite a change from the wagon. My two youngest sister sat with our parents, while Ruby and I sat on boxes at their feet. If it was cold, mother would heat a couple of flat irons, wrap them well and place them down by our feet. Lap robes were also used to protect us and them from the chill. Even then we sometimes got real cold before we reached our destination. It was a different story in the summer and the women learned quickly to make themselves linen dusters to keep the flying dust off their clothing.

Buggies were still used a lot, even after cars began coming in. Yes, I had many dates in a buggy!

A two seated buggy, properly called a surrey, next gained some popularity. The fancier ones had fringe all around the top. I remember one Fourth of July when we left home in our surrey at daylight, as it took so long to get into town. People came from every part of the county as patriotism ran high those days. I can still see all the vehicles lined up and the horses tied to the chain link fence, which went around the square, next to the courthouse lawn.

Barton Countians were fortunate for we had a wagon and carriage works right here in the county seat. Gustavus Seyffert, a native of Saxony, Germany, came to Lamar in 1866 when there were only 12 houses here, and opened a shop to make these vehicles on the very spot where Gilkey's Ford agency now is. For a time this was the largest business establishment here, as he hired eight men.

The two train lines were hauling passengers by the mid 1880's and were a means of transportation used by many. My first trip was to Sheldon and back and what a thrill that was! We seemed to go so fast!

I remember so well the first car I ever rode in. It was a one-seated, doorless Ford owned by my mother's brother, Sam Lee. Riding in it made us feel like we were almost flying. It was such a change from riding in a buggy or surrey.

A little latter, another brother, Rob, got a two seated Ford. These cars were open, so the passengers and driver got the full effect of the breezes. It wasn't long until someone thought of side curtains which could be snapped on, and thus keep out some of the bad weather.

Many citizens bought cars and it wasn't long until there were quite a number here. For instance, down Kenoma way Jap Songer got a 1909 Oldsmobile; Lou Arft was the proud owner of a 1909 or 1910 Maxwell; Dock Kline bought a Buick; Charles Young got a 1909 Ford and Riley Harris purchased an Overland.

For years, people told this story on Mr. Harris. He was learning to drive and managed to get the car inside the garage but he forgot how to stop it. He kept yelling "Whoa! Whoa!" But it took the back wall to stop it. So he had two doors cut in the back end. When he wanted to drive in, he opened all the doors. That way, it could go right on through if he couldn't stop it.

Here in Lamar, my uncle John Earp purchased a Reigle which he kept padlocked, so his son Guy couldn't sneak it out. F.D.W. Arnold, owner of the Pickwick Hotel, bought a 1915 Winton; Colonel C.Y. Trice got an Oakland and hired Paul McLaughlin to drive for him. One day Paul and my Charles decided to go swimming. On the way, they ran into a flock of chickens and one hit a headlight so hard it broke the glass and lodged inside the light.

There were many similar tales told those days about the citizens and their experiences with these new fangled machines.

Buses came into existence about the time we got decent highways. For many years, they did a thriving business carrying passengers, but today, few ride them. As a result, the bus lines are having a struggle.

Next came small airplanes and it was hard for people to accept the idea of flying through the air. The first ones were open cockpit, windy and noisy. For several years one would come to our Fair, when it was still being held at the old fair grounds, and take passengers for a short ride over the town. I believe they charged 25 cents per person. Only the dare devils took advantage of this opportunity.

A good many years later, I did get up the nerve to ride over the eastern part of Kansas City with Ben Gregory, one of the city's foremost fliers.

Never in my wildest dream did I ever think I would some day fly over the Atlantic Ocean in a huge TWA plane, but I did. What a thrill to fly above the clouds going over and coming back home. I won't say I wasn't nervous!

Then the astronauts flew to the moon, landed and two even walked on it - another giant step in transportation. My Grandmother Lee, who died in 1946, often told me the time would come when people would fly to the moon and thinking nothing of it. That day may come yet, but it is one I won't participate in, due to my age.

And so, just in a lifetime, we have progressed from horse-back to space ships. I wonder what changes are in store in the next 50 or so years.

One Couple Made A Lasting Impression On Reba When She Was Twelve

August 18, 1990

All kinds of people can be found in a town the size of Lamar. Some make quite an impression on us as we are growing up, while others we soon forget. One such couple was Henry and Tishie Beeker. If you ever knew them, you remember them.

When I was about 12 years old, we lived on Maple Street between 8th and 9th in a place we knew as the Tuma House. I think I remember this name so well, because I always thought it such an odd one.

South of us a few houses, but on the west side of the street, was a small old-time cottage occupied by this couple known as Henry and Tishie Beeker.

The 1911 county directory lists Henry as a railroader, but Edith Klein remembers him well as a street cleaner. She said she could just see him with his broom and cart sweeping the square. So, he evidently changed jobs as he got older.

Both were mentioned as Baptist in a 1913 booklet published by the church at that time.

They did not fit into the usual mold of married couples. We girls often wondered why in the world they ever married. He was a small built, wiry type fellow and Tishie was a tall, raw-boned woman with a severe countenance. We weren't quite sure how to take her when we first moved on the street.

They weren't mated in temperament either, for we could hear them fussing any time of the day or night. We often wondered what happened to cause such "knock-downs and drag-outs."

We learned later that Henry was real tight with his money and wouldn't even give her a nickel to buy a spool of thread. So, she decided she would make a little money for herself by taking in a few washings.

I remember so well how she looked when she took the clean laundry home. She was always careful to fold each piece neatly and put it in her basket which she then placed in her little red wagon. In cold weather, she always wore her long, heavy wool sweater over her ankle-length dress and on her head she had a close fitting wool cap tied under her chin with strings. Down the street she would trudge, rain or shine!

Tishie finally got tired of such a life, so she bought a lot a few doors north and had a comfortable little home built. I'm sure she didn't expect Henry to move in with her, but he did. Affairs would run along smoothly for a while and then there would be another big argument. At these times, we'd see Henry and a few belongings moving back to the little house where he'd stay until he got so lonely for Tishie that he would move back to the new house. I wouldn't venture a guess as to how many times we saw him move back and forth.

Once in a while, I'd go over for a visit but I was never quite sure how to take her or him, either.

A few years later she had heard that my sister, Dode, was planning to marry Johnny Miller, who was half German. She stopped by our house one day and told her she shouldn't marry a German, for if she did, she'd regret it the rest of her life. We decided Henry must be that nationality or she wouldn't have made such a statement. We never found out for sure. Fact is, Dode and Johnny had many happy years together.

I purposely neglected to tell you that Tishie painted the entire front of her house with red roses. That made it a conversation piece for sure and many drove by just to see a house with a rose garden across the front. Even Authur Aull, editor of the *Democrat,* was impressed and gave her a nice write-up.

Now that I think back, I wonder if this was one of the ways she used to get attention, for goodness knows, she likely got very little from Henry or perhaps from anyone else, for that matter.

Joys Of Childhood

November 21, 1990

I often wonder if today's children have the fun we had when we were growing up. Many children rush in from school and turn on the Television to catch the late afternoon programs. There are exceptions, I know, but I do believe most of today's children are watchers and not do-ers. I can't help but wonder what this will do to their creative development. Since we didn't have Televisions or radios to entertain us, we had to make our own fun; we never seemed to lack things to do, either.

This season of the year always reminds me of the happy hours we spent in the woods gathering nuts. We always hoped to find a hickory nut tree or two, as we preferred their nuts to those of the black walnut; they were easier to pick out and were so delicious in cakes, cookies and candies. I don't remember that we had many pecan trees around those days. We also kept an eye out for a persimmon tree and were happy when we could take some home. We learned early when to tell if they were ripe and when they might be bitter!

Those days, families did things together. Thanksgiving Day was such fun, for we all piled into the wagon and went to one of our grandparents for the feast. Sometimes we went to our Great Grandmother Howell's near Milford. That is where I saw the little pig roasted and on the center of the table with a red apple in its mouth. How we did enjoy playing with our cousins, the Wes Lee children, for we didn't see them very often.

Then there was the annual Fourth of July celebration and the Fair to attend. Some children got to go to the Jerico Springs Picnic on June 10, but we never had that opportunity.

We always looked forward to the Christmas celebration and especially the one at the church. The Sunday school parties were a lot of fun, particularly after we were old enough to "like the boys." Every summer, the churches and the lodges often had ice cream socials, which were a treat to us.

We could hardly wait for one Saturday night to the next. Practically every person in the county attended the concerts held at the bandstand. When we were quite young we would watch for Cecil and Wilma Bruce, who came in from Bushnell; we would chase each other around a big tree and have fun in general. Little did we dream that this was the very tree that the mob used to hang Helper after his murder spree at Kenoma.

I wonder if children today play a lot of games, both inside and out, as we did. Our two favorites for inside were Fruit Basket Upset and Hide the Thimble. After we grew a little older, we often played Post Office at our parties. We young folks thought this game somewhat risque'; I don't remember much about it now, but it seems the winner got to kiss the boy or girl, as the case may be, of their choosing.

Drop the Handkerchief, Hide and Seek, Jump the Rope, Hop Scotch and Tag were the outside favorites for us girls. The boys preferred Baseball and Ante-Over.

About April 15 of each spring we began begging to go barefooted, knowing all the time we wouldn't be allowed to before May 1. What fun it was to walk in mud puddles and have the black "stuff" squeeze up between the toes!

We loved the spring, for besides going barefooted, we spent hours picking wild violets and the pretty lavender Sweet Williams. They made such pretty bouquets. Later in the summer we picked white clover blooms and sat for hours making chains to wear around our necks. Sometimes we made crowns for our heads and bracelets for our arms.

We four sisters each had our own shoe box in which we kept our paper dolls. They had been cut from Sears or Wards catalogues, and from fashion plates gotten at the local dry goods stores. We had families of them who would visit each other.

Sometimes we'd take rocks and make a house in outline form; large rocks were tables and chairs, and pieces of broken dishes were the utensils. Mother often said we'd play so long and hard that she would have to check on us.

I spent many pleasant hours reading. When I was eight, I read Black Beauty (horse) and Robinson Crusoe all the way through. A neighbor lady told mother I wouldn't be bright if I didn't quit reading so much.

When families got together the men would discuss current events and especially politics. I recall in particular the 1908 Presidential campaign when William Jennings Bryan was making another of his attempts to become president and the discussion was quite hot. I always wondered why he lost every time. Maybe my interest in politics goes back to those entertaining discussions which I always tried to listen to.

So, you see, life was far from dull for us children.

I hope everyone has a good Thanksgiving dinner, but, I bet not one of you will have a roasted pig with an apple in his mouth right in the middle of the table. I can see that pig yet!

Truman Birthplace Today 1992, Lamar, Missouri.

"Grandpa Earp" and "Uncle Everett Earp Standing in front of President Truman's Birthplace.

Wyatt Earp's Relatives Once Lived In Truman Birthplace

January 14, 1991

When I was growing up, a small, white, two-story house stood at the northwest corner of what was then 11th and Kentucky streets. Across the street south was the Franklin Ward School, which Reba Griffin (Streeper) and I attended. We were in the fourth grade and Miss Mattie Martin was our teacher.

I'm sure it never entered Mr. Simon Blethrode's head when he was driving in all those nails back in 1882 that he was building a home in which a future president would be born.

He sold the home, when completed, to John and Martha Young Truman, where baby Harry S. was delivered by Dr. W.L. Griffin (no relation to Reba) for the big sum of $15. The baby was born in the tiny southwest bedroom, hardly large enough to whip a cat in, on May 8, 1884.

I'm sure no one here ever dreamed that this baby would grow up to be active in national politics and eventually be the 32nd man, but the 33rd president of our great nation. It was when he became well known that Kentucky Avenue was changed to Truman Avenue, as it remains today.

In 1920, my grandparents, Walter and Emma Earp, purchased the Truman birthplace. They had been living out east on 160 highway where Joe Wilson now lives, but grandma's health was failing and they needed to live where her work was lighter.

Little did they realize that a prominent fellow Democrat had been born in this house.

Wyatt's father, Nicholas and grandpa's father, Jonathan - a Southern Methodist minister were brothers, which made Wyatt and grandpa first cousins. The family was very proud that Wyatt had been appointed constable when the village was organized in 1870. This, in fact, was Wyatt's first law job.

The last time I visited with grandpa, we sat on the porch swing and he told me of their move here from Montgomery county, at Uncle Mick's insistence; how he and Adelia (Wyatt's sister) were playmates, as they were near the same age, and what he thought of the rest of the family. He said he especially admired the handsome Wyatt.

In the meantime, one of the several owners between the Truman's and the Earp's occupancy had built a porch across the front and added a kitchen off the northwest corner of the house, both of which changed its appearance a lot. Grandmother used the present kitchen for a sort of combination dinning and sitting room.

We four girls stayed with them a lot and helped with the work. We washed many tubs of clothes on the board and did the big baskets of ironing; also we scrubbed the floor - the very floors the Trumans had walked on. We even helped grandmother make her preserves and jellies. Two of my favorites were her pickled crabapples and her relish, which she called piccalilli. She usually served these in her oblong shaped dish, which had a lion's head at each corner. I own this dish now.

Grandpa saw to it that we helped him keep her garden clean; a job we all four hated. If I remember correctly, the garden was in the same spot where the administrator has her old time garden today.

I'm sure there was a fence around the backyard, and I think I remember them having a cow; most townspeople did keep a cow back then for the family milk supply.

Two of us sisters at a time stayed with our grandparents to help them. She was getting quite frail, but was always nice to us.

We slept in the south bedroom upstairs. It was cooler, for where the south window is now, there was a door which let in cool breezes. If it was terribly hot, we slept on the floor in front of the door.

Since I was teaching, I couldn't help as much as the others did. I did my share on weekends, and during the summer, though.

Grandmother passed away on February 15, 1923, in the very room where Mr. Truman first saw the light of day. Her funeral service was held in the little parlor with many spilling over into what was the grandmother's dining room.

Grandpa died in the other downstairs bedroom on December 21, 1945. son Everett and wife, Marie, then took the house over. The family was so pleased when they received a telegram from Mr. Truman at grandpa's passing away. He seldom came to Lamar without calling on grandpa for a short visit.

Everett was determined that the birthplace would become a memorial to the President, even though the Trumans had moved away when the baby was 10 months old. He couldn't seem to convince people that this should be done. Even the city fathers, Chamber of Commerce, and the average citizen dragged their feet a bit about putting up signs to the highway, and also erecting a sign outside the house stating it was the President's birthplace.

So, Everett put them up himself. I've often wondered if the city wanted to put up more permanent ones. People were already stopping to see the room the President was born in.

If you remember Everett, you know his nickname was "Big Chief." He was proud of the fact he was related to Wyatt, and also that he himself had been local constable for 12 years. He also had the habit of stretching things a bit. Few knew he sent loads of coal to people without heat, as well as baskets of food for the hungry, for he never bragged about his good deeds.

The United Auto Workers bought the home from Aunt Marie after Everett's death in 1956. The dedicated it to the state of Missouri, and it is now under the jurisdiction of the State Park Board. It is now on the National Register of Historic Places, Department of the Interior. I often think how happy Everett would be if he knew his dream had been fulfilled.

The home brings many visitors to Lamar today. This past year there were people from 45 states and eight foreign countries, according to Rita Embry, administrator.

I'm sure Mr. Blethrode would be shocked if he could know that a President was born in this little house; also that relatives of the popular Wyatt Earp, who had a major part in the opening of our west, had called this place home for over 30 years.

We just never know what might happen, do we?

Local Historian Recalls Famous Citizens Of Barton County

February 2, 1991

Most of us old timers know about the famous people from our county, but I doubt if those of you who have moved here in more recent years are familiar with this information.

For instance, do you know that one of our presidents was born in the small white house at the northwest corner of 11th and Truman? This street was originally Kentucky, but was renamed

after Harry S. Truman became president, following the death of President Franklin D. Roosevelt. I daresay there are people living here at present who have never visited the home, which is now a historic shrine and is open to the public free of charge.

The president had an older baby brother, also born here, who is buried at Lake Cemetery. Turn right at the first road going east. On the north side of the road, just before reaching the turn to the north, is a little stone which has engraved on it, "Baby Truman."

During World War II, three local

Harry S. Truman

men served their country in an outstanding way. Rear Admiral Selby Combs, Brother-in-law of Zetta Mae Combs, was com-

mander of naval air craft in the southwest Pacific and later was commander of the aircraft carrier, the Yorktown. I recall how thrilled I was when I saw this huge vessel tied up in New York harbor, knowing that Selby had once been its commander!

Charles A. Lockwood was vice admiral, commanding the Pacific Submarine Fleet during the same war. The former Lockwood home stands on the west side of Gull street. If you go west on 8th street, you will run into it, unless you

Selby Combs

Freeland Daubin

turn north or south. Both Admirals Lockwood and Chester Nimitz had the honor of representing the U.S. Navy aboard the USS Missouri on September 1, 1945, at the formal surrender of the Japanese.

The third admiral from here was Freeland Daubin, son of Crittenden C. Daubin, County treasurer here many years; my mother was his deputy. Freeland was commander of the U.S. submarine forces in the Atlantic. Dorothy Stratton, a renowned educator, grew up in the Golden City-Mt. Carmel-Kenoma area. During World War II, she was director of the Women's Reserve-Coast Guard, with the rank of it commander.

Dr. Harlow Shapley was born and grew up in the southwest part of the county, near Nashville. Early in life he showed an interest in astronomy and went on to add many degrees to his title. He eventually became known as the most famous astronomer in the world. Dr. Shapley was the first to give logical argument that life exists elsewhere in the cosmos. When visiting family here, he often taught an adult Sunday school class at our United Methodist Church.

Charles A. Lockwood

Tracy Richardson, known as the world's greatest machine gunner, was born in Lamar in 1890. He was known as a soldier of fortune and participated in several revolutions in South American countries. During World War I, he served in the Canadian, British and U.S. Air Forces, and during World War II was an infantry instructor at Fort Benning, Georgia, among other assignments. Wounded at least 16 times, he returned to Lamar to live out his life with his sister, Miss Leila, in the home where Carl Bartlett now lives. He was both a national and an international figure and was idolized by younger men. I recall that Mr. Aull always gave him such interesting write-ups when he came home to visit. He died in April 1949 and is buried in Lake Cemetery.

Wyatt Earp is another of our former citizens who is widely known for his skill with a gun and for the part he played in helping open the west. Those days it was shoot or be shot, though he preferred using his fists or a club rather than a gun. He got his start in law work right here in Lamar with the first board of trustees, appointed after the village's incorporation in 1870, made him city marshal. As he moved on west, he held various law offices.

Eventually, he and his brothers, along with others, were able to clear Arizona and surrounding states of cattle rustlers. Many statements concerning Wyatt are untrue; yes, he had many enemies. He disliked all the publicity and before he died said, "After I'm gone, I hope I get the peaceful obscurity I haven't had during life."

Another famous figure here was Arthur Aull, editor and publisher of the *Lamar Democrat* from August 8, 1900 to his death in 1948. In 1901, his paper became a daily, which was unique for a town the size of Lamar, Missouri. Since he published a paper like no other, it grew rapidly and soon had subscribers from coast to coast. People liked his unusual skill with words, his printing of the facts as he saw them and his witticisms. Remember his columns "Bill Spivens and Mandy," and the "Haybalers?" He was

Arthur Aull

widely quoted and *Life, Times* and *Harpers* wrote him up extensively. Many tried to hire him, but, as he said, "I prefer to be my own boss."

So, these are just some of our Barton County people who became famous in their chosen fields - both here and in foreign lands. Do you suppose any other county in the U.S. can meet our record?

Other Important List In Barton County Is Also Lengthy

February 21, 1991

I didn't forget these important people, as some of you may have thought. The February 2 article was getting a bit long, so in order not to leave anyone out, I decided to just do another article.

Can you imagine a local man establishing a new town which was known as the most unique in the United States? It was for free thinkers only. The man responsible for this unusual village was a lawyer by the name of George Walser, who came here following the Civil War. He served as our prosecuting attorney as well as two terms in the state legislature, and also practiced law in the county.

While living in Lamar, he became interested in the works of Robert Ingersoll, and atheist. He helped form a small group of non-believers here, but the local Christians made life so unpleasant that he went down the tracks about 18 miles, bought some land, and created this little town which he called Liberal. It ranks as one of the oddest in the history of this country as it was to be a refuge for those who had different ideas and beliefs.

In his advertising pamphlet, he said, "Liberal is a town with no priest, no preacher, no church, God, saloon or hell." In 1883, a barbed wire fence about one-fourth mile long was erected to keep the Christians and the infidels apart.

Interest in free thought began to wane in 1886, so Mr. Walser joined the small group of spiritualists who had settled there, and later became a very active member. In fact, he developed beautiful Catalpa Park about a mile south of Liberal where many spiritualist gatherings of people in this country as well as from other countries were held. In the 1890's, five international conventions were held in this park.

At age 60, he divorced his second wife and married a young medium, who later became mentally ill and poisoned herself in a Joplin hotel room.

The fourth wife insisted he move to Lincoln, Nebraska. While living there, the man who had been an agnostic espousing free thinking, and later a spiritualist, next became a Presbyterian. His interest turned to writing and to botany and he published, "The Life and Teachings of Jesus," as well as three volumes of poetry about flowers.

On May 1, 1910, he was caught in a sudden rain storm and developed pneumonia. The last wife would not allow his burial in the cemetery he had planned at Liberal, and had a mausoleum built just east of the main entrance to Lake Cemetery at Lamar, where their remains are today.

So the man who could have had a brilliant law career in Lamar became known throughout the United States and Europe for the queer causes he became aligned with and not for what he really accomplished in life.

Have you ever heard of a young man by the name of Levi Morrill who moved here right after Civil War where he fought with the Kansas 7th Calvary? He was a graduate of Bowdoin College and was a contemporary of Longfellow and Hawthorne, as well as a protege of Horace Greeley at the *New York Tribune.* He practiced law here, and along with Truman Powell established a newspaper call *The Lamar Advocate.*

He married a Miss Jennie Dickerson here and both a son Oscar, and a daughter, Susie, were born here.

One fall, he went on a hunting trip to the Ozarks with friends and was so taken with its beauty that he came home, sold his interest in the paper to his friend Truman Powell and moved his family and belongings in three wagons to this land of beauty, after living here just 18 years. He later became the Postmaster at Notch, near where Silver Dollar City is now.

In 1895, he befriended another Easterner who in 1907 published the book *"Shepherd of the Hills,"* using the people near by as characters. Levi Morrill became Uncle Ike in the book and Susie, the daughter, was Sammy Lane. Some say this book ranks next to the Bible in the number who have read it.

Because Ike was the oldest postmaster in the United States, he was called to Kansas City by the Chamber of Commerce to dedicate the first air mail service between Kansas City and St. Louis. He never fully recovered from the tiring trip and died three months later on August 22, 1926, the day after his 89th birthday. Both he and Sammy Lane are buried in the "Shepherd of the Hills Cemetery," about a mile down the road from the old post office. The last I knew the old post office is still standing and is listed in the National Register of Historic Places.

This is a brief story of one of Barton County's former citizens who became known over the U.S. and a large part of Europe. When I was in England for three weeks, I was amazed to find they knew about the book and even who Uncle Ike was.

When I was a little tyke, we lived for a time at the east end of 6th street on the north side of the road. I often noticed a school boy walking by on his way to high school. He always carried his lunch and an arm load of books.

I soon learned his name was John Brown and that he lived east of Milford, where his father was a miner. He lived with George and Fanny Isenhower and was working for his board and room so he could go to high school.

One of his duties was to look after the livestock. In order to be near the livestock at night, they made him a room in the barn where he slept and studied when not doing chores.

Ruby Weidman told me recently that the town kids rather ignored him at first for he didn't have as nice clothes as they had.

This class, including John, graduated in 1912 and guess who was valedictorian. Yes, it was the little country boy they had once ignored. He also won the Hake Medal, given by Bill Hake, the jeweler. This medal was for the highest scholastic record that year and was the beginning of a long line of medals given by the Hakes. I understand John made the highest grade average of any student graduating up to that time.

From here, John worked his way through Rolla Schools of Mines. He was determined to become a geologist and sure enough he became a national authority on the subject. He was also in demand overseas and especially in South American countries.

In 1962, the class of 1912 had it 50th reunion. John and his wife Evangeline, attended. I'm sure it was his last visit here. By the way, Sis Martin and Ruby Weidman are the only class members alive so far as they know.

So, this student who had a room in a barn and whose clothes were not as stylish as the "town kids" ended up with a summer home in New York State, lived in Washington, D.C., and was a world authority in geology with the title of mining engineer.

This makes 12 people who were known in many countries, all from Barton County. There may be others, but I'm not aware of them.

Riding In Rumble-Seat Was A Thrill For Youth

April 1991

Have you ever ridden in the rumble-seat of a car? To ride in the back, as well as in the open, was a thrilling experience for young people when these cars were popular.

The first car equipped with the rumble seat that I remember was a 1928-29 Model A Ford. About then, Henry Ford realized he must improve his Model T, and so after much experimenting and many dollars spent, he came out with the Model A. Among these was a sports roadster with a rumble seat which sold for $480. Then he also manufactured a sports coupe with a canvas top over the front seat and a rumble seat in the rear. It retailed for $550.

These weren't Ford's first attempts to make a car with a rumble seat, however. In 1907-1908, he came out with a roadster that held at least three people. One passenger rode in a rear seat separate from the main body, which was often called the "mother-in-law" seat. It was indeed a crude looking car by today's standards.

In 1909, he made a closed coupe, also with a so-called rumble seat. These early ones didn't close, so were always out in the elements.

I've often wondered why they dropped the idea for a number of years, as they did.

Country roads weren't paved yet, so dirt was a real problem. Passengers wore goggles and duster coats made of linen to help keep the dust off. The wind played havoc with our hair, no matter if it was still long or had been bobbed. If dad hit a mud puddle a little fast, you could expect to look like a speckle freak afterward.

I heard once of a little boy who was afraid to ride across the creek near their house because of the steep banks. He was sure he'd fall out, and a time or two he did.

Other car manufacturers began making some rumble seats on their roadsters and coupes. About 1930, or a little earlier, the Auburn roadster appeared, and soon the Willis Knight roadster was also on the market, and around 1935 the Dodge Coupe came out, all of which had rumble seats.

The rear end of these cars with the rumble seats resembled today's trunks. To open, a handle near the top was pulled down to reveal a leather upholstered seat which held at least two people.

I'm not clear as to how we got up into the rumble seats at the rear of these new fangled cars. Some say there was a step-up from the running board onto the fender and from there one stepped into the seat. Others insist they stepped onto the bumper first and then onto the fender before stepping into the seat area. Either method got you into the seat and ready to take off. By the way, fenders were much heavier those days than they are now.

Young people preferred riding in the back, for then they could sing the popular songs of the day as loudly as they wanted to without fear of disturbing the adults in the front. Kate Smith's song, *"When The Moon Comes Over The Mountain"* was sung over and over. Other favorite were, *"I'm Forever Blowing Bubbles,"* and *"Life Is Just A Bowl Of Cherries."* Since cars weren't enclosed, the passengers got the full benefit of the engine noise as it crawled over the rutted earth. It was next to impossible to talk from the rumble seat to anyone in the front. One young man took advantage of this and proposed to his sweetheart. She accepted and they spent many happy years together.

These cars weren't built very many years, for there were too many undersirable features. The young folks enjoyed them though while they were in style.

There are some nice features about being older, for one has many pleasant memories younger folks will never have.

My thanks to Jewell Medlin, a former Ford dealer, for all his help in supplying me with information for this article.

Feed Sacks
Once Had Many Uses
June 1, 1991

So many have reminded me that so far no article about feed sacks has been in the *Democrat.* I'll admit that many times I've thought about those pretty sacks with flowered designs, but for some reason, I just couldn't seem to get an article written.

I daresay the younger generation today would have difficulty realizing that fee for the animals on the farms ever came in these cloth sacks.

The first task of the housewife after one became empty, was to remove the string, resulting in a good size piece of cloth; It was put in with a chain stitch and was difficult to undo unless one pulled the correct string first. This string was next wound around a ball of twine, which mother kept in a cupboard drawer. All packages those days were put in a paper sack and tied with a string. Therefore, we saved every bit we could for future use.

The sack was then opened up and shaken vigorously to remove any loose contents. Next came the washing and ironing before they were neatly folded and put away until needed. It was common practice to take them to the women's meeting at the church, or to sewing circle, where the ladies traded around until they had several of the same pattern and could then make something they needed.

For years, our little daughter slept in nightgowns made from pretty sacks. She also wore dresses and petticoats made out of them. Can you imagine the little girls of today being happy with such outfits? Our children knew no better.

Baby bibs were practically all made from them. Some mothers even made diapers when money was to scarce to buy regular diaper material.

One large sack made a nice lunch cloth for the kitchen table. Several sewn together served as a good backing for the new quilts which mother had pieced.

I have even seen kitchen sash curtains and valances made from sacks. They were quite attractive, too. I believe my favorite use was for tea towels, for they were absorbent as well as colorful. Then I've seen them used to strain milk or apple juice when making cider.

One lady I knew made window shades. Another early day common use was to spread one over the bread dough, which had been placed in the old tin dough riser, and then put on a chair behind the heating stove to rise.

I'm one of those old fashioned women who likes to wear a cobbler type apron over my dress when I'm doing my work. (I don't wear slacks.) For years I made these out of feed sacks. I have only two left and won't likely have any more. They have gone up from 25 cents to $3.50 or more. I don't really like man-made materials--the kind we have today. There is no end to the way sacks were used. No doubt, you have heard your elders speak of many more than I have mentioned.

Some youngsters have been known to ask what we did before we had plastic wrap, foil, Elmer's glue, paper towels, and plastic bags. They are told about these feed sacks, as well as the smaller flour and sugar sacks. They are still puzzled thought, for they have never heard of feed or food coming in cloth sacks.

What a different world we live in today!

Orphan Trains
Once Stopped In Lamar

August 1992

Never can I forget the two orphan trains that came through Lamar when I was young. At least a number of the children came from Dr. Wann's Presbyterian Orphanage by way of the New York Foundation Home. The plan was to find decent homes for them and see that they had enough to eat.

One morning, my father took my sister Ruby and me down to the depot to see one of them pull into the station. How I did worry about those children! We were poor ourselves, but I couldn't imagine anyone being as poor and neglected as those little ones where.

I could just visualize how frightened they were, for they had no idea what was going to happen to them.' There ragged clothes were removed before they reached Lamar, Missouri. They were then given clean ones and instructed not to get them dirty.

While both these trains were headed for Lamar, we met the one at the Frisco depot. I'm not sure about the other one.

As I recall it, the children were taken to the Opera House and lined up so everyone could see them well. Each adult hoped to find one that especially appealed to him or her.

There was a Mr. and Mrs. Givens in our church who were childless. Mr. Givens was a baker on the west side of the square. They hoped they might see a child that appealed to them, but instead of seeing one, they saw a boy and his two sisters. I recall the boy's name was Ross, but that of his two sisters has long been forgotten.

Would you believe that years later, when we lived in Kansas City, I purchased two axminster throw rugs at Jones Store and Ross was the salesman who waited on me. What a thrill this was! In recent years I have heard that he now lives in Carthage, Mo. I keep hoping I'll run into him or his sisters.

The foster parents died years ago, but not until they had gotten the three children reared. I've often thought how fortunate they were to get to stay together with such kind, good people to rear them.

Another little three year old boy was taken by a Mr. and Mrs. Claude Rogers. They saw that he had a good education and he later was considered one of Phalow and Phalow's best abstractors. He also served in the Adjutant General Department of the Army when Mr. Truman was our president. It was his responsibility to help the President serve medals to those earning them in the service.

He later passed away at the age of 47. His wife is now one of my good friends.

Some people took children for the work they could get out of them and not for any likely affection. Some children went from home to home, never feeling secure or loved.

Phyllis Wright remembers three little girls who lived out Iantha way. They were Dorothy Hayes, Evon Gibbs and Lottie Givens. She never knew if these were their real names or if they were names given by the people who took them.

I've often wondered if Alfrieda Smith of Jasper was on one of these trains, but I guess I'll never know.

A Long Life Yields View Of A Unique Way Of Life

September 30, 1992

One cannot live close to 100 years without having many experiences that the average person today has not ever had, and perhaps never will.

We had to walk across a pasture to meet the Alf Whitaker kids with whom I rode to school. My father always walked with me, and we had to cross the pasture which had many Indian mounds where Indians were buried. These graves were decorated with bright pieces of broken glass, which the Osage Indians, who lived rather close by, placed there each year for decoration.

My father used an old fashioned walking plow to till the soil. We children followed and tried to see who could gather the most and the prettiest.

Mr. Kemp, who had an Indian show, often let some of his Indians come over and visit my father. We children played around their pant's legs and had fun, just as small children do.

One day, papa came screaming out of the barn with a snake hanging onto him. He had been gathering eggs from a nest in the barn loft and the snake didn't like his feeding place disturbed. Since it was a non-poisonous snake, no harm was done.

I shall never forget seeing the big platter on the center of the table at Thanksgiving at my great grandmother's house. On that platter was a small roasted pig with a red apple in its mouth. I had never seen such a sight before. By the way, I own that blue platter today.

When we were little girls, our parents took us to the ice cream suppers at Milford. These were always held in the vacant lot between Frank Faubion's General Store and Ed Boles' Grocery. We children really enjoyed these ice cream suppers. I recall one time I played so long and hard with the Werts' kids that papa wouldn't let me stay long enough to have a bowl of ice cream. So, I went home without any. Papa's word was law those days, and even though my heart was broken, I didn't get any.

We had just had our dinner, and we children were playing horse on the wagon wheels. Mama came to the door with a basket holding a few clothes and told me to come and get them for the house was on fire. I was given the job of keeping my little sisters on the wagon wheels and away from the fire. I remember screaming for my mother to get my new straw hat and our recently purchased gramaphone horn. I got neither.

Since we four little girls were left with very few clothes, the Milford ladies met at Grandma Lee's and made panties and pinafore type dresses for us out of various kinds of sacks.

We always went to Sunday school and took part in the programs. We liked to march round and round singing, *"Bringing in the Sheaves!"* That was my favorite.

Those days no one had kitchen cabinets, so we set our food on the shelves with a curtain hanging in front of them to keep the dust out. This particular time we went to Nashville to visit our Lee grandparents and the jellies, etc. were left on the shelves. Lo and behold, when we got home, there was a mouse head down in the pitcher! To this day, I can't eat white Karo.

Do children today have similar experiences? I doubt It!